D1449443

Pictures and Words

Animals

Pictures and Words
Animals

written by Carolyn Jackson

Franklin Watts
A Division of Grolier Publishing
New York   London   Hong Kong   Sydney
Danbury, Connecticut

Produced in association with Media Projects Incorporated

Editor and Writer: Carolyn Jackson
Managing Editor: Lelia Mander
Assistant Editor: Aaron Murray
Designer: Laura Smyth

For Franklin Watts: Douglas Hill, Senior Editor
                    Susan Ferrelli, Photo Researcher

Library of Congress Cataloging-in-Publication Data

Jackson, Carolyn (Carolyn D.)
    Animals / by Carolyn Jackson
        p.   cm. — (Pictures and words)
    Summary: An illustrated encyclopedia of animals, with separate sections covering
mammals, birds, reptiles, fish, mollusks, crustaceans, amphibians, insects, and arachnids.
    ISBN 0-531-11712-X (lib.bdg.)   0-531-16437-3 (pbk.)
    1. Animals Encyclopedias, Juvenile. [1. Animals Encyclopedias.]
    I. Title.   II. Series: Pictures and words (New York, N.Y.)
    QL49.J1355   1999
    590'.3—dc21   99-24959
                                                            CIP

Photo credits:T=top, B=bottom, C=center, L=left, R=right
Cover: © Image Technologies: mountain lion, lizard, zebra, gorilla.
Interior: © Mark Adams/Westlight: 54BR; © Roger and Donna Aitkenhead/Animals, Animals: 42B; © Miriam Austerman/Animals,
Animals: 34B; © Erwin & Peggy Bauer/Bruce Coleman, Inc.: 75C; © Fred Baverdam/Minden Pictures: 103B; © Bill Beatty/Animals,
Animals: 91B; © M. & E. Bernheim/Woodfin Camp & Associates: 19; © George Bernard/Animals, Animals: 11B; © Victoria de
Bettencourt/Animals, Animals: 15B; © Jim Brandenburg/Minden Pictures: 58T; Bruce Coleman, Inc.: 74TR; © Joyce
Burek/Animals, Animals: 105C; © Jane Burton/Bruce Coleman, Inc.: 107T; © Joe Cancalose: 63C; © M.C. Chamberlain/DRK Photo:
76B; © Daniel J. Cox/Natural Exposures: 40; © Stephen Dalton: 13T; © Peter David/Planet Earth Pictures: 104; © Adrian
Davies/Bruce Coleman, Inc.: 120B; © Tim Davis/Photo Researchers, Inc.: 25B; © Tui De Roy/Minden Pictures: 57B; © E.R.
Degginger/Animals, Animals: 105TR; © E.R. Degginger/Photo Researchers, Inc.: 108; © Phil A. Dotson: 51L; © Rick
Edwards/Animals, Animals: 35B; © Richard Ellis/Photo Researchers, Inc.: 57T; © Michael Fogden/Animals, Animals: 13B; ©
Michael Fogden/Bruce Coleman, Inc.: 52; © Adrienne T. Gibson/Animals, Animals: 61T; © Mickey Gibson/Animals, Animals: 79;
© George Grall/National Geographic Image Collection: 100L; © Jack S. Grove/Tom Stack & Associates: 62B; © F.J.
Hiersche/Photo Researchers, Inc.: 78; © Henry Holdsworth: 18R; © Henry Holdsworth/The Wildlife Collection: 55L; © Image
Technologies: 20B, 23, 24 (both), 27, 28 (both), 29, 31B, 33L, 43, 45B, 47, 53T, 54L, 54TR, 56B, 58B, 59R, 86, 90B, 92 (both), 110
(both), 111B; © Mitsuaki Iwago/Minden Pictures: 35T, 61B; © Johnny Johnson/Animals, Animals: 37L, 55R; © Johnny Johnson/Tony
Stone Images: 59L; © Wolfgang Kaehler: 88; © M. Philip Kahl/Bruce Coleman, Inc.: 84T; © Breck Kent/Animals, Animals: 22B,
109TR; © Mitch Kezar/Tony Stone Images: 10; © Rudie Kiuter/Oxford Scientific Films: 100R; © Frank Krahmer/Bruce Coleman,
Inc.: 72; © Stephen J. Krasemann/DRK Photo: 17B; © Gerard Lacz/Animals, Animals: 109L; © Frans Lanting/Minden Pictures: 26,
37R, 41, 81T, 84B, 96T; © Bill Lea/New England Stock Photo: 17T; © Tom & Pat Leeson: 65; © Tom & Pat Leeson/Photo
Researchers, Inc.: 49B; © Zig Leszczynski/Animals, Animals: 96B; © R. Ian Lloyd/R. Ian Lloyd Productions: 60; © Robert
Maier/Animals, Animals: 16 (both); © Mohn Markham/Bruce Coleman, Inc.: 107B; © Maslowski/Photo Researchers: 83L; © Joe &
Carol McDonald/Tom Stack & Associates: 63T; © Mark W. Moffett/Minden Pictures: 114; © Flip Nicklin/Minden Pictures: 101,
103T; © David Northcott/DRK Photo: 89B; © Stephen Parker/Photo Researchers, Inc.: 119B; © Andrew Plumptre/Oxford Scientific
Films/Animals, Animals: 32B; © Fritz Polking/Peter Arnold Inc.: 20T; © Michael Quinton/Minden Pictures: 44B; © Leonard Lee
Rue/Animals, Animals: 48; © Runk/Schoenberger/Grant Heilman Photography: 11T; © Herb Segars/Animals, Animals: 105BL; ©
Michael Sewell/Peter Arnold Inc.: 76T; © Anup Shah/Photo Researchers, Inc.: 36; © John Shaw/Tom Stack & Associates: 93; ©
Claude Steelman/Wildshots: 46L; © Stock Market: 113; © Kim Taylor/Bruce Coleman, Inc.: 123B; © Larry Ulrich/DRK Photo: 121;
© Doug Wechsler/Animals, Animals: 97B, 122L; © L. West/Photo Researchers, Inc.: 115; © Fred Whitehead/Animals, Animals:
94R; © Art Wolfe: 74L, 75B, 80 (both); © Shin Yoshino/Minden Pictures: 62T

© Franklin Watts
All rights reserved.
Printed in the United States of America and Canada
1 2 3 4 5 6 7 8 9 10 R 08 07 06 05 04 03 02 01 00 99

How to Use This Book

There are millions of animals on Earth. We've chosen about 175 for you to learn about. All of them live in the wild. Choosing which animals to include was not easy. We chose some animals because many people want to learn about them. We chose others because most people don't know about them. Some are plentiful. Others are very rare. They may be endangered. That means there are fewer and fewer of them living in the wild. This book is a good place to begin to learn about animals. Here are some clues to help you:

■ The animals are divided into groups. Mammals and Reptiles are two of them. Other groups are listed in the Table of Contents.

■ Animals with an entry to themselves are listed under their groups in the Table of Contents. The lists of animal entries are in A-Z order. For example, Camel is listed in the Mammal group. It comes after Buffalo.

■ Some animals do not have an entry of their own. Swordfish are a part of the entry on Saltwater Fish. You can find them and many other animals in the Index at the back of the book. The Index is in A-Z order by subject.

■ Some entries tell you to go to another page to learn more. These are called cross-references.

■ The Glossary gives the meanings of words about animals and science that you may not know yet. You can tell if a word is in the Glossary because it is shown in bold type.

■ Pictures can tell you what animals look like and what they do. Be sure to read the words under the pictures. They are called captions.

No matter where you begin, we hope you will use this book again and again. After all, people are animals, too. See page 10.

Table of Contents

MARSUPIALS and MONOTREMES

Table of Contents, continued

MAMMALS

**Mammals produce milk to feed their babies.
Almost all mammals give birth to live young.**

Mammals are smart

Mammals have bigger brains than other animals. People are mammals. They are the only mammals that can think about life itself, and talk about their thoughts. But other mammals are very smart. They have many ways of showing who's boss without killing each other.

Read more about **Lions** on page 37.

At home in many places

Mammals have some control over the heat of their bodies. This is why they are can live in so many places. In cold places, most mammals have lots of fur to keep them warm. They may also have layers of fat that hold heat. When it's hot, most mammals sweat. Special glands give off water to cool their skin.

Some mammals, like woodchucks and groundhogs, take a very long nap in the winter. They **hibernate** for months. They live off the energy stored in their fat until springtime, when they wake up.

In very hot temperatures, some mammals shut down, or **estivate**. They move very slowly or stay in one place to save energy and keep cool.

ARMADILLO

Armadillo means "little armored one" in Spanish. This mammal lives in grasslands and forests.

Where do armadillos live?

Most armadillos live in Central and South America. Only one kind, the nine-banded armadillo, lives in the southern United States. Scientists think there could be 50 million nine-banded armadillos. Another nineteen kinds of armadillos live in Latin America.

Nine-banded armadillos can actually have 7 to 11 bands.

A coat of armor

Armadillos have five plates that protect their bodies. These are located on their heads, backs, tails, and both sides. The plates are hard, like a turtle's shell. The bands in the middle of the body move like a telescope. Soft skin connects them to each other.

Carbon copies

Armadillos mate in July and August. The babies don't start to grow in the female's body until November. Then, in March, two, three, or four identical babies of the same sex are born.

What's for dinner?

Armadillos feed at night. They eat lots of insects, small reptiles, and amphibians. Sometimes they eat birds, small mammals, fruit, the kill of other animals, or even garbage.

BABOON

Baboons are monkeys that live on the ground in many parts of Africa. They walk on all fours.

All different sizes and colors

The largest baboons are dark gray. Their bodies can be nearly four feet long and weigh ninety pounds. Their tails are about three feet long.

The smallest baboons are reddish brown. They can be less than two feet long. Their tails are shorter than their bodies. Even these baboons can weigh thirty pounds.

Hamadryas baboons have rough hair and bare bottoms. Males have wide manes and side whiskers. The males weigh about forty pounds.

A baby baboon rides on his mother's back.

Troops on the march

Baboons travel together. Crossing a rocky plain, a troop of fifty baboons will gallop along, sniffing the air. The strongest males stay in the middle. They have the largest teeth. Mothers and young baboons travel with them. Young adult males guard the edges, where cheetahs may be waiting to attack.

Do baboons fight?

It's not wise to fight a baboon. Mostly, they eat plants, scorpions, and small animals. But at night they might raid a farm for lambs. They may attack humans if they feel threatened.

Baboons have strong jaws.

BAT

Bats are the only mammals with real wings. But they have no feathers. Skin connects their arms and feet.

Where do bats live?

Bats can't stand the cold. Some bats **migrate** 800 miles to escape winter. Most bats live in **tropical** climates. But some live in **temperate** North America. They may even live in the attic of a house in your neighborhood.

Bats fly at twilight and at night.

Are there really vampires?

Most bats eat insects. Some eat fruit. A few eat meat and fish. Vampire bats in South and Central America drink blood. They make a shallow bite in the skin of a sleeping cow, horse, or goat. Then they quickly lap up some blood and fly away. Once in a while, bats bite people. Some bats carry disease.

Just hanging out

Mostly, bats live in caves and trees. Since their feet are connected to their wings, walking is hard. Hanging upside down by their claws is easier. Bats use their claws to cling to twigs, branches, walls, and ceilings.

White bats huddle together as they rest.

BEAR

Bears are big, heavy mammals with loose skin and shaggy fur. Their faces have long snouts.

Grizzly bears

Grizzly bears once roamed North America from Mexico to Alaska. Today, they live only in national parks of the United States and Canada. Grizzlies can be nine feet tall on their hind legs and weigh up to 900 pounds. Their brown fur has white tips.

Grizzly bear

Do bears hibernate?

Females give birth in winter while other bears take a long sleep. Normally, we say they **hibernate.** But it isn't true hibernation. That's because a bear's body temperature stays high. On mild winter days, bears may wake up and take a walk.

Polar bears

Polar bears got their name because they live near the North Pole. Their white fur makes them hard to see on the ice and snow. Polar bears even have fur on the bottoms of their feet. This keeps them from slipping on the ice.

Polar bear

Beware of bears!

Bears have five toes on each of their four paws. Each toe has a long heavy claw. A bear can kill a person with just one paw swipe. Bears like to be alone. They have short tempers, so beware!

BEAVER

Beavers cut down trees with their four front teeth. Using their front feet like hands, they build homes.

How big are beavers?

Adult beavers are about four feet long with their wide, flat tails. They eat a steady diet of marsh grass, roots, barks, and twigs. Some weigh seventy pounds.

Fur keeps them warm

Beavers have soft, thick fur next to their bodies. Their darker brown top coats are longer and rougher. Beavers groom their fur with the claws on the inside of their webbed back feet. Oil glands near the tail help keep the beaver's fur waterproof and shiny.

Family life

A female gives birth to three or four babies every year. A beaver family has two parents and several offspring under two years of age. Each spring, just before the mother gives birth, the father moves out of the lodge for a while. The two-year-olds move out, too. They look for mates to share the rest of their lives.

Beavers cut down trees to build dams and lodges.

BOAR

Boars have large heads with long, round snouts and two sets of tusks. Their hides are thick and hairy.

Global beasts

Boars and their kin live in more parts of the world than any other large mammal. Explorer Hernando de Soto brought the first pigs to North America in the 1500s. The wild razorbacks in the Southeast descended from them.

Even a heavy sow can trot and canter.

Rooting around

Boars dig food from the ground with their sharp tusks and long snouts. They also eat lizards, frogs, small birds, and even rattlesnakes.

Pig tales

Many people have mistaken ideas about boars and their farm cousin, the pig. They are not naturally fat. They do not sweat. They are not dirty. They wallow in the mud to cool their bodies. Mud also protects boars from the sun and from lice. Boars and pigs are smarter than dogs and cats.

This baby boar will grow to be as big as a large man. It will be a fast runner and a good swimmer.

BOBCAT and COUGAR

Bobcats and cougars are North American cats. Cougars may be six feet long. Bobcats are much smaller.

How do bobcats hunt?

Bobcats live mostly in the South, in mountains and along the coast. They hunt rabbits, rats, birds, and sometimes white-tailed deer. They sneak up on their **prey**. Then they pounce with their sharp claws. Bobcats have short jaws and long canine teeth.

Cougar

How do cougars hunt?

Cougars feed on large animals, mostly deer. They hunt alone at dawn, dusk, and night. A cougar will wait quietly. Then it will leap onto an animal's back and break its neck. After eating part of the animal, the cougar may go away, then return to finish its meal later. Hunting cougars is legal in eleven United States and two Canadian provinces.

What do you call a cougar?

Cougars are also called catamounts, mountain lions, panthers, and pumas.

Cougars everywhere

Humans are the only large mammals that live in more American places than cougars. Cougars live in North, Central, and South America. They live in forests, jungles, mountains, and deserts. Sometimes they even wander into cities.

Bobcat

17

BUFFALO and BISON

Buffalo and bison are kinds of wild cattle. Only one kind, the Asian water buffalo, has ever been tamed.

Home on the range

The animal many call the American buffalo is really a bison. Huge herds of these shaggy beasts once filled the plains and **prairies**. Native Americans depended on them for food and leather. Hunters with guns almost killed them off. Today, the bison is coming back.

About 2,000 bison live in Europe. The rest live in North America.

Dependable workers

The Asian water buffalo pulls plows and does other heavy work for people. Water buffalo are also raised for their milk, meat, and hides. They live in India and Southeast Asia.

What do they eat?

Buffalo and bison eat only plants— and lots of them. If they live on the plains, the animals eat grass. If they live in the woods, they eat leaves.

Where buffalo really roam

Buffalo are wild cattle with big horns. The largest African buffalo weigh almost 2,000 pounds. The normally peaceful African buffalo are very dangerous when wounded.

CAMEL

Camels are plant-eating animals with one or two humps on their backs. They live mostly in the desert.

Is anyone thirsty?

Camels can go for months without drinking water. They store water in their humps. These are mostly fatty tissue. Camels can lose up to one-fourth of their body weight in water before they have to drink. When they are thirsty, their humps may sag.

Camels in America?

The first camels probably lived in North America about 10 million years ago. They spread from there to other continents. Camels have been **extinct** in North America for 2 million years.

One hump or two?

The dromedary is a camel with one hump. People of the Middle East tamed dromedaries about 5,000 years ago. They rode dromedaries across the desert, drank their milk, and ate their meat. They used camel hair for clothes. They used the hides for tents. They burned camel manure for fuel.

Bactrian camels have two humps. Their coats are long around the heads and the tops of their front legs and tails. Bactrians are gentler than dromedaries but have been tamed only half as long. They live in Central Asia. Some Bactrians are still wild.

Dromedaries live closely with people.

CHEETAH

The cheetah is the world's fastest animal. It can run 50 to 70 miles per hour in short spurts.

Day hunters

Cheetahs are among the smallest of the big cats. They weigh between 80 and 140 pounds. Speed is their biggest advantage. Unlike many animals, cheetahs hunt by day. They hide in the tall grass of the African savanna and wait for their **prey**—antelopes, impalas, wildebeests, and zebras.

After running to catch its prey, a cheetah may have to rest half an hour before it eats.

Some zoos are breeding cheetahs.

Cheetahs are endangered

Cheetahs once lived in Europe and North America, as well as Africa and Asia. Today, less than 15,000 cheetahs live in **tropical** Africa. A few survive in southern Asia.

Cheetahs have beautiful spotted coats. Hunters killed many cheetahs for their furs. Now scientists know another reason for the small number of cheetahs. At the end of the last Ice Age, about 11,000 years ago, scientists believe there were probably only about ten cheetahs left. Today's cheetahs are their descendants.

CHIMPANZEE

Chimpanzees are the closest living relatives of human beings. In the wild, they live only in Africa.

Close, but not the same

Scientists believe that chimpanzees and humans shared a common ancestor more than 6 million years ago. Today, their **genes** are very much like ours, but still different. Chimpanzees' brains are smaller than ours, and the shape of their vocal chords makes it impossible for them to speak.

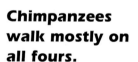

Chimpanzees walk mostly on all fours.

Fruit eaters

Chimpanzees' favorite food is fruit. The sweeter it is, the better they like it. Chimpanzees also eat nuts, termites, and small animals, such as monkeys. Chimpanzees use plant stems to get termites out of their mounds. They use stones and sticks like hammers to break open nuts.

How big are chimps?

There are four kinds of chimpanzees altogether. Three kinds are almost as big as humans. They live mostly in forests. The fourth kind, pygmy chimpanzees, also known as bonobos, are smaller. They live in the **rain forest**.

Endangered species

Chimpanzees are in danger of dying off or becoming **extinct**. People keep cutting down trees from their forest home. Illegal hunters, called poachers, capture them to sell or kill them for meat. Today, the chimp's worst enemies are its human kin.

CHIPMUNK

Chipmunks are small, reddish brown animals. They have dark and light stripes on their faces and bodies.

Big teeth

Chipmunks are related to squirrels. Like squirrels, they have four big front teeth. These teeth are used for gnawing and chewing. The chipmunk must use its teeth to keep them worn down.

Furry tails help chipmunks keep their balance.

What do chipmunks do all day?

You may see chipmunks scurrying around trees. They can climb if they need to, but usually they stay on the ground. There, they gather nuts and seeds. They stuff food into little pouches inside their jaws. Then they carry it underground. They sleep underground most of the winter.

Baby chipmunks

In the spring, the female chipmunk gives birth to three, four, or five babies. These babies grow very fast. By fall, they are fully grown. Chipmunks don't live very long. Larger mammals, reptiles, and birds like to eat them. But because they grow and have babies so quickly, chipmunks can survive.

This sleeping chipmunk has wrapped itself in its long tail.

COYOTE

Howling, yapping coyotes live in Mexico and the southwest United States. Their cries carry a long way.

Coyote or wolf?

Coyotes are wild members of the dog family. They are about half the size of wolves, but their ears are bigger than wolves' ears. They are very smart. And they can run fast, too. Coyotes mate for life.

Big ears help the coyote hear better.

Town or country?

Coyotes live throughout North America. They may even wander near a big city. They eat almost anything, including garbage. They kill rabbits, deer, and **rodents**. They also eat insects and fruit.

Family life

Female coyotes give birth to about six pups in the spring. The pups leave home after six to ten weeks.

Fair game?

Farmers and ranchers dislike coyotes because they kill sheep and other farm animals. But the coyote eats dangerous rodents. This controls disease and saves crops.

A coyote hides in the grass as it hunts its prey.

DEER

Deer have lived near humans since prehistoric times. Early humans hunted deer for food and for their hides.

What are antlers?

Antlers are a deer's main defense.

Antlers are fast-growing bone. They grow in springtime and fill out in winter. While they are growing, they have a soft covering called velvet. Except for female reindeer, only males have them. Deers shed their antlers every year. A new, larger set grows in. Antlers help the deer fight off **predators**. Males also fight each other with their antlers.

More and more, every year

In North America, most deer are whitetails. There may be 20 million. That's probably more than ever before. Once, wolves and cougars ate white-tailed deer. Today, dogs are their main natural predator.

Where do deer live?

Once, most white-tailed deer lived in woods east of the Mississippi River. Today, they live in wetlands, dry lands—and suburbs.

Forests were the deer's original habitat.

Garden pests

Deer eat grass, twigs, and tree bark. They also eat garden vegetables.

DOLPHIN and PORPOISE

Dolphins and porpoises are not fish but air-breathing mammals. They are actually small whales.

What do they look like?

Dolphins are more streamlined than porpoises. Also, they have sharp teeth. Their snouts look like beaks, and their top fins are hooked. Porpoises have rounded snouts, and triangular fins. Their teeth are shaped like shovels.

Snouts on porpoises are less pointed than on dolphins.

Killer what?

Orcas, or killer whales, are the largest dolphins. They are black and white with about fifty cone-shaped teeth. Each tooth is three inches long. Orcas are called killer whales because they kill other big animals. No wild orca has ever been known to kill a person. Orcas often hunt in groups, called pods.

How do they communicate?

Dolphins and porpoises are very smart. They "talk" to each other in squeals or whistles. Some scientists have tried to learn the dolphin language. Both dolphins and porpoises use a kind of sonar. They send out sounds from an oil-filled organ on their heads. When these sounds bounce back, the animal knows what's ahead of it.

Dolphins learn to hunt by frolicking.

ELEPHANT

After whales, African elephants are the largest animals. Some are twenty-five feet long and thirteen feet tall.

What's a trunk for?

Elephants breathe, smell, touch, eat, and drink with their trunks. Elephants also use their trunks for cuddling. Trunks include long noses and a top lip. There are also little "fingers" on the side. Elephants' trunks are strong and flexible. They use them to strip leaves and branches from trees.

Asian or African— which is which?

There are two kinds of elephants: African and Asian. African elephants' ears are twice as big as Asian elephants' ears. The largest Asian elephants are smaller than the largest African elephants.

A large, thirsty elephant can drink 40 gallons of water a day. Elephants squirt water into their mouths with their trunks.

Big appetites

Elephants are plant eaters. To stay alive, they must spend many hours of the day eating. Elephants in circuses and zoos eat about 150 pounds of hay daily. They eat bucketsful of other food.

A wild male elephant may need 500 pounds of food a day. Elephants travel in herds of ten to fifty animals. Imagine what they do to a forest!

Long ago, there was plenty of space for elephants. They ate and moved on. The trees and grass grew back. Today, as people settle more land, elephants have fewer places to live. In Africa, parks have been set aside for elephants. But they are too small. Also, because of hunting, elephants are in danger of becoming **extinct**.

Hard workers

Asian elephants are often tamed and put to work. In India, they work with loggers in forests. Long ago, they were taken into battle. Today, most circus elephants are Asian. They rarely forget a trick.

Elephants have been hunted for their tusks. The ivory was used for piano keys and medicine. It is illegal to hunt elephants today.

Where does ivory come from?

Elephants grow long, curving tusks. Tusks are huge teeth that grow out of the elephant's top jaw. They are made of bony material called ivory. Asian male elephants have tusks. Both male and female African elephants have them. Males fight with their tusks.

27

ELK and MOOSE

American elk and moose belong to the deer family. Moose are the biggest members of that family.

The shaggy moose

Moose have long legs, large heads, and big muzzles under their jaws. Another long flap of skin hangs under the throat. It is called the bell. Male moose are called bulls. They are often ten feet long and more than seven feet tall. And that's not counting their huge, spoon-shaped antlers. The antlers may be six feet wide.

American elk

Waders and grazers

Moose feed on willow, poplar, and birch trees. They often wade into lakes to eat water lilies.

Who's who?

Moose are larger than elk. American elk are grayish brown and about five feet tall and eight feet long. Their antlers are five feet wide. They live in Canada and the Rocky Mountains. Moose live in Europe, Asia, Alaska, Canada, and the northwest United States.

This animal is called a moose in North America and an elk in Asia and Europe.

Fox

Foxes are the smallest members of the dog family. They have long, slender bodies, short legs, and bushy tails.

Growing up fast

Fox puppies are usually born in late winter. They can't see at first and open their eyes after ten days. For six weeks they drink their mother's milk. Over the summer, they learn to hunt. By fall, they are living on their own. After their puppies leave the den, the adults split up. Each takes its own territory.

Foxes may be red like this one. They may also be gray, brown, or white.

No picky eaters here

Foxes like meat best, but they eat almost anything. Foxes run, jump, and swim to catch their **prey**. The gray fox can climb trees. Foxes eat rabbits, birds, and small **rodents**, such as mice and chipmunks. They also eat fruit and the remains of animals killed by other animals. Sometimes they attack farm chickens.

Different kinds of foxes

Red foxes may grow to be twenty-two pounds. They are the largest foxes. They live in North America, Europe, Asia, and North Africa. Fennecs are the smallest foxes. They weigh about three pounds. They live in the desert in North Africa and Arabia. Their large ears give off heat. Arctic foxes have thick white coats that hold in heat.

GAZELLE, GNU, and CHAMOIS

Gazelles, gnus, and chamois are all members of the antelope family.

Where do gazelles graze?

Gazelles run like deer, but they live like cattle. Wild gazelles graze in herds on open plains from central Asia to North Africa. Others live in eastern and central Africa.

The graceful gazelle

The tallest gazelles are less than three feet high. Most gazelles have beautiful black-ringed horns. Their coats are brown or tan with black and white marks.

Big gnus!

Gnus (it is pronounced like "new") are also called wildebeests ("will-de-beast"). They live on the plains of Africa. Gnus have manes, beards, and thick, curved horns. They can weigh 600 pounds. They may be more than six feet long and four and a half feet tall.

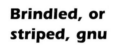

Brindled, or striped, gnu

Soft-skinned chamois

Chamois ("sha-mwa") live among the mountain rocks of Europe and western Asia. Their horns grow straight up and back. Chamois are about four feet long and weigh less than 100 pounds.

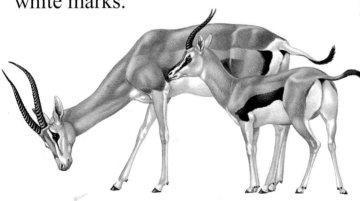

Grant's gazelle (rear) is bigger than Thomson's gazelle.

GIRAFFE and OKAPI

No animal is taller than the giraffe. Males are eighteen feet high. A tall female is about three feet shorter than the male.

Clever disguises

Giraffes live on the grassy African savanna. Their coats are yellowish with darker patches. There are nine kinds of giraffes with nine different patterns. The patterns help them hide from lions.

Okapi cousins

Okapis do not look like giraffes, but they are closely related. They live in African **rain forests**, where they eat fruits, seeds, and leaves. They have tall necks and large

Okapi

ears. Their tongues are long enough to wash their eyes! Unlike the giraffe, the female okapi is taller than the male. She may be five and a half feet tall.

A giraffe's horns are covered with skin.

Leaf-chompers

Giraffes eat the leaves of many trees. With their thick lips and long tongues, they pluck leaves, flowers, and fruits from around the thorns.

Who eats giraffes?

Adult giraffes have only one **predator**—the lion. Sometimes, though, a big giraffe can kick a lion to death. Lions, cheetahs, leopards, and crocodiles all eat baby giraffes.

GORILLA

Gorillas are the largest of the great apes. Males are sometimes six feet tall. Females are much smaller.

What do gorillas eat?

Gorillas are vegetarians. They spend most of their days looking for food. They walk on all fours using their knuckles. At night, young gorillas and females with babies may sleep in nests in trees. They rarely fight. When males compete, they usually beat their chests.

Silverhaired males

Mature adult male gorillas are called silverbacks because the hair on their backs is silver. Most silverbacks live with several adult females and some black-backed males and younger gorillas.

Silverback

Young gorillas stay with their mothers about three years.

Rain forest dwellers

There are three kinds of gorillas today—the western lowland gorilla, the eastern lowland gorilla, and the mountain gorilla. All three live in the African **rain forest**. Because the gorillas' **habitat** is shrinking, some people think they may only survive in protected places like zoos.

GROUNDHOG, GERBIL, and GUINEA PIG

Groundhogs, gerbils, and guinea pigs aren't pigs at all. They are rodents, like squirrels and mice.

Groundhogs

Groundhogs, also called woodchucks, live everywhere from Alaska to Alabama. These animals are chunky with short legs. They have rough brown fur on top and pale undercoats. They eat wild plants and farm crops. In winter, groundhogs **hibernate**, or go into a deep sleep. Groundhog Day is February 2. Legend says that if a groundhog sees its shadow on that day, there will be six more weeks of winter.

A groundhog looks out of its burrow.

Cuddly balls of fur

Guinea pigs are furrier than groundhogs or gerbils. Their fur may be white, black, or brown. It may be streaked or

Guinea pig

spotted. Guinea pigs' natural home is in the Andes Mountains of South America. They lose their baby teeth before they are born. They breed and grow up very fast.

Popular pets

Wild gerbils and guinea pigs don't live in North America. But many people keep them as pets. Most gerbils have long tails. Their back legs are also long. Wild gerbils live in Asia and Africa. The popular pet comes from Mongolia, in Asia.

HIPPOPOTAMUS

The word hippopotamus means "river horse."
But its closest living relative is the pig.

African giants

Hippopotamuses are the largest land mammals after elephants. They are short and very heavy. The largest weigh about 8,000 pounds. Long ago, hippos lived in India, Europe, and Africa. Today, hippos live only in Africa.

At home in water

Hippos live near rivers and lakes. Baby hippos are born in the water. They nurse underwater. They can swim right away. Adult hippos can hold their breath for about ten minutes. They walk around underwater and look for plants to eat. Hippos have huge mouths with three sets of tusks. They could crunch a basketball in a single bite.

Hiding out

Most of the time, hippos walk away from a fight. They hide in the water with just their eyes, nostrils, and ears sticking out. If a more powerful animal comes along, the hippo may spread dung on it by flapping its tail. People once thought that hippos could sweat blood, but they don't. Their mucus glands give off a pink oil.

Among mammals, only the whale has a mouth larger than the hippopotamus.

HYENA and JACKAL

Hyenas look like dogs with long hind legs. Jackals are smaller than hyenas. Both are related to dogs.

Spots and stripes

There are three kinds of hyenas. The laughing hyena makes a noise like a human laugh. It laughs during mating season and when it is excited. This animal has a grayish yellow coat with dark spots. It weighs about 180 pounds and lives in central and southern Africa. The striped hyena and the brown hyena are smaller. The striped hyena lives in India and Southwest Asia as well as Africa. The brown hyena has a gray head and legs with brown stripes. It lives in South Africa.

A yawning hyena shows his powerful jaws.

Tough jaws

The hyena's jaws are so strong that the hyena can carry the body of a gnu in its teeth. It can crush the bones of cattle. Hyenas kill living animals, and they also eat dead ones.

The jackal's howl

You can hear jackals howl for miles around. They hide in the day and hunt at night. They eat small mammals, chickens, and dead animals. Jackals live from central Asia to South Africa.

Black-backed jackal

LEOPARD

Leopards are the smallest big cats. Lions, tigers, and cheetahs are bigger. Yet leopards are the most fierce.

Fine fur

Leopards' handsome fur helps them hide. They usually have yellowish brown coats with both large and small black spots. (Panthers are leopards, too. They have spots, but it is hard to see them.) People hunt leopards for their skin. Hunting has made some kinds of leopards rare. Leopards are protected in many places. Other countries have passed laws against selling leopard skins.

A leopard takes a break before finishing its meal.

Many homes

Leopards live in grasslands, mountains, and jungles. They attack from trees. They jump on passing cattle, sheep, antelopes, monkeys, dogs, and birds. Leopards are found in many parts of Africa south of the Sahara. They also live in Asia and the East Indies.

The non-leopards

Two big cats called leopards really are not. The snow leopard has a heavy gray or cream-colored coat. It lives in the highlands of Central Asia above the treeline. The clouded leopard is yellow with black spots and blotches like clouds on its sides. It lives in Asian forests.

LION

The lion is often called the king of the jungle. With their thick manes, male lions even look kingly.

Group tactics

Lions eat mostly zebras and antelopes. They hunt in groups. Female lions do most of the killing. They hide in the grass or bushes. The males drive the **prey** toward them. Then the females spring out and attack. Lions have strong muscles and sharp claws.

A group of female lions rests after a kill.

The lion family is called a pride.

Baby lions

Lion cubs are born about 110 days after their parents mate. There are two to six cubs in a **litter**. At birth, they are the size of small house cats. Cubs have spots and stripes that fade with time.

Where do lions live today?

Lions once lived in Europe, Africa, and Asia. Today, they live in protected parts of Africa and India. African lions live mostly in open country. The 175 remaining Asian lions live in India's Gir Forest.

LLAMA

Llamas live in the Andes Mountains in South America. Their coats of long, fine wool keep them warm.

Surefooted

Llamas' feet have two toes. Each toe has a padded bottom and a long, curved nail on top. Llamas are sure-footed. They were once wild, but they have been pack animals for about 4,000 years. Llamas are related to camels. Llamas don't have humps, though. They are also related to alpacas, vicunas, and guanacos of South America.

Llama language

Llamas hum when they are curious or upset. If they sense danger, they give a high-pitched call. And if they are threatened, they spit. You can tell when a llama is relaxed. Its ears are forward. If it is worried, its nose tilts up and its ears go back.

How do llamas eat?

Llamas eat mostly hay. They also eat bushes and other plants. Their stomachs have three parts. After they chew and swallow their food once, it passes into the first part of their stomachs. It is digested a bit and then comes up as cud. The llama chews this before swallowing it for good.

MONKEY

Monkeys are hairy animals with long legs and tails. There are many kinds of monkeys. They are all smart.

New World monkeys

New World monkeys live in Central and South America. They include woolly, howler, spider, and squirrel monkeys. Marmosets and tamarins are New World monkeys, too. New World monkeys are graceful and slender. Their nostrils are far apart and open to the sides. They live in trees.

De Brazza's monkey

Old World monkeys

Old World monkeys live in Africa, Asia, and southern Europe. Their nostrils are close together. Baboons, macaques, langurs, and colobus monkeys are all Old World monkeys. Their rumps have pads to sit on. Some live on the ground. Most Old World monkeys have hands that work like human hands. Almost all monkeys use their tails like another arm to grip tree limbs.

Group life

Monkeys live in groups. Some are small, with just a male, female, and their offspring. Other groups have 300 monkeys. Monkeys eat leaves, fruits, grasses, insects, eggs, bats, birds, and small reptiles. They must always look for food. Living in big groups makes this easier.

Hanuman langur

OTTER

Otters are furry mammals with thick tails. They have claws and webbed feet, and they live in the water.

Playing and eating

Even grown-up otters are playful. They slide down banks and splash in the water. In India, some people train otters to drive fish into their nets. Otters often eat while swimming on their backs. They use their bellies as tables. Otters like to eat fish, crabs, sea urchin, clams, or oysters. They crack shells with their big teeth. Or they might use a rock.

Where do otters live?

Most otters are freshwater otters. They live in rivers and lakes and are born in dens at the water's edge. A female gives birth to two or three babies in early spring. She carries them on her back until they can swim. The sea otter lives in the ocean. Sea otters are born one at a time. They live in beds of seaweed in the North Pacific.

An otter rests in a bed of seaweed.

Dangers

Hunters kill otters for their thick, dark fur. They have the thickest fur of any mammal. It is made into fur coats for people. Water pollution has killed many otters, too. It also kills the sea life they eat.

PANDA

There are two kinds of pandas, the giant panda and the red panda. They live in Asia.

What's the difference?

Giant pandas are black and white. They have small black ears and large black patches around their eyes. A giant panda can weigh up to 270 pounds. Red pandas are much smaller. They are rust-colored, with cream-colored bands around their tails. The largest weigh about thirteen pounds. Red pandas spend most of their lives in trees.

A giant panda eats bamboo.

Bamboo for dinner!

Both kinds of pandas eat bamboo plants and live in the forest. A giant panda may need eighty-five pounds of bamboo a day. Sometimes it eats other plants and some meat. Giant pandas have bones that stick out of their wrists. These help the panda hold its bamboo. The panda has powerful jaws and large, flat molars. These teeth crush the tough bamboo.

Not enough space or food

Pandas are **endangered**. Their **habitats** are shrinking. They are running out of food. There are only about 1,000 giant pandas left in the world. Almost all of them live in six small mountain ranges in China. A few pandas live in zoos around the world.

PORCUPINE

Porcupines are rodents that make their homes in the woods. They live alone in burrows and hollow trees.

Watch out for those quills!

Porcupines move slowly and clumsily on their short legs. Their sharp quills are their best defense. Cougars know to turn porcupines over. They attack porcupines' soft bellies.

New World porcupine

Quills for protection

Porcupines don't shoot their quills. Instead, when the porcupine shakes its tail, the quills come loose. When an animal touches a porcupine, the quills stick into it. Every quill ends like a fishhook. They can grow up to four inches long.

Bark eaters

Porcupines come out at night to look for food. Their sharp claws help them climb trees. With their long front teeth, porcupines feed on the bark of trees. Aspens and birch trees are their favorites. Sometimes they eat so much bark that they can kill the tree. New World porcupines live in North and South America. Old World porcupines live in Africa, Asia, and southeast Europe. They cannot climb trees.

Furry babies

Female porcupines give birth to one baby at a time. The babies have soft fur. Their quills are only one-half inch long. Porcupines will grow to about forty pounds.

PRAIRIE DOG

Prairie dogs are related to squirrels, but their bodies are heavier. Don't confuse them with marmots or woodchucks.

Woof!

You can recognize prairie dogs because they bark. The fur of prairie dogs may be yellow, brown, or red-gray. It isn't as soft as it looks. Their legs and tails are short. Like all **rodents**, prairie dogs have big front teeth. They have to keep chewing.

Town life

Prairie dogs are very social. Thousands of them live together in prairie dog towns. These towns fill the **prairies** of North America. You can't see them, though, because the towns are underground. The entrance tunnels may be ten feet deep. Prairie dogs live in groups called coteries. They have one male, one to four females, and their young under two years old. Many coteries form a ward. Several wards make a town.

A prairie dog looks around.

No friend to farmers

Farmers and ranchers dislike prairie dogs. Their horses sometimes fall into prairie dog **burrows** and break their legs. Also, prairie dogs eat crops and grasses needed for grazing cattle. Many prairie dogs have been killed as pests. The one place they can live safely is a national park.

RABBIT and HARE

Rabbits and hares have long ears and short tails. They run and leap with their powerful back legs.

Rabbits are usually smaller than hares.

A lot alike

Rabbits and hares have two sets of long front teeth. They have a smaller set of teeth behind these. Both animals eat grass, leaves, buds, and twigs. They feed at dawn, dusk, and night. You can't always tell a hare by its name. Jackrabbits are hares, for example.

A snowshoe hare nibbles a pussy willow.

The most common rabbit

Cottontails are the biggest group of rabbits in the Americas. They live from southern Canada to South America. When they are fully grown, cottontails weigh up to four pounds. Most rabbits nest above ground, but cottontails use **burrows**. They use holes dug by other animals. Most hares dig their own burrows.

Lots of babies

Rabbits and hares multiply fast. Females may give birth to four to seven **litters** every year. These litters have up to eight babies. Baby rabbits are furless and blind. Baby hares, however, have fur and open eyes.

RACCOON

Raccoons are furry animals with long ringed tails. Their dark masks make them look a bit like bandits.

What do raccoons eat?

There are seven kinds of raccoons. They live all the way from southern Canada to South America. Raccoons eat garbage or farm corn and chickens. In the wild, they eat fish, lizards, birds, and insects. They also eat fruit and berries. Crab-eating raccoons have shorter fur and legs than other raccoons. They live in Central and South America. Some raccoons live only on small islands off Florida and Mexico. Still others live in the West Indies.

Pioneers sometimes made hats of raccoon skins.

Raccoon myth

Some people have noticed raccoons washing their food before eating it. Are raccoons naturally clean and tidy? Only captive raccoons wash their food. Scientists think they do this to imitate catching food in the wild.

Most raccoons are loners. They stay with their mothers only until they can hunt for themselves.

At home in the trees

Raccoons live in forests and grasslands near water. They avoid high **altitudes** and dry places. Raccoons spend most of their time on the ground. But their homes are often high in trees. They are good climbers.

RAT and MOUSE

Rats are larger than mice. There are brown rats, black rats, pack rats, and muskrats. There are many kinds of mice, too.

Why so many?

There are billions and billions of rats and mice. This is because they breed year-round. Female house mice mate when they are forty days old. They give birth twenty days later. Each **litter** has four to seven babies.

Rats and mice use their sharp front teeth all the time, for gnawing and chewing.

Friends to scientists

Scientists often experiment with rats. The rats used in laboratories are often all-white, or albino, specimens of brown rats. These rats have helped people learn about nutrition, genetics, and disease.

Dangerous and dirty pests

Rats and mice are **rodents**. They have four big front

Australian water rat

teeth—two on top and two on the bottom. They cause much damage with their teeth. They harm farm crops. They ruin food. They also spread disease. The black rat spread a terrible plague throughout Europe 650 years ago. One out of four people died from the disease.

Today, the brown rat yearly destroys hundreds of millions of dollars in food.

Black rat

Sometimes called the Norway rat, it probably first came from Asia.

REINDEER and CARIBOU

Reindeer and caribou are different names for the same animal. They belong to the deer family.

What do caribou eat?

Caribou live in herds. They travel all the time, looking for food. They eat mostly lichen and the bark of small trees. They have broad hooves with sharp edges. These hooves help caribou move in snow, ice, and watery bogs. Sharp hooves help them dig out food. Large male caribou may be seven feet long and weigh 660 pounds. At the shoulder, they are five feet high.

Antlers for him and her

What is called a caribou in North America is called a reindeer in northern Europe and Asia. Both males and females have antlers. They are long and slender with branching points, called tines.

Migrating herds

Some caribou **migrate** long distances. They travel all the way from the Arctic to spend winter in Canada's forests. Oil pipelines in Alaska were designed so that caribou could pass under them to feed. Woodland caribou don't go as far. They live in bogs and forests in the Pacific Northwest and western Canada.

The people of Scandinavia and Siberia use reindeer as work animals.

RHINOCEROS

**Rhinoceroses are heavy, plant-eating mammals.
They can't sweat, so they stay in mud to keep cool.**

Hunted for their horns

Rhinoceroses have horns on their heads. Rhinos use them to dig and to fight. Some people think rhino horns make strong medicine. Hunters have killed most of the rhinos for their horns. More than nine of every ten rhinos have disappeared since 1970. All five kinds of rhinos are **endangered**.

African rhinos

There are two kinds of rhinos in Africa, the black rhino and the white rhino. Both are brown-gray. And both have two horns.
The white rhino is the world's largest. It can weigh four tons, or 8,000 pounds.

Asian rhinos

The three kinds of Asian rhinos are the Sumatran, the Javan, and the Indian. Asian rhinos have one horn. The heavy skin of Asian rhinos looks like armor. It is one piece of folded skin. There are only a few hundred Sumatran rhinos and less than 100 Javans. Only about 2,000 Indian rhinos are living today. They are found in northeast India and Nepal.

Rhinos are near-sighted. They can see clearly only 30 feet away.

SEA LION

Sea lions bark. They sound more like dogs than lions. Their young are even called pups.

Flippers for feet

Some people confuse sea lions with their close relatives, the seals. Sea lions have small ear flaps. Seals have no ear flaps at all. And sea lions are usually smaller than seals. They get around much better on land than seals do. This is because sea lions can turn their front flippers around to help them walk. Sea lions can swim very fast. Sometimes they jump out of the water like dolphins.

Male sea lions, called bulls, are much larger than females, or cows.

Where do sea lions live?

The largest sea lions, called Steller, live in the Northern Pacific. They are big—sometimes weighing more than 2,000 pounds! Sea lions also live on the west coasts of North and South America and on the coasts of Australia and New Zealand. Once, there were sea lions in Japan. But too much hunting drove them away. Besides hunters, the sea lion's enemies are orcas, or killer whales, and great white sharks.

A group of female sea lions is called a harem.

49

SEAL

In the water, seals are graceful. They are clumsy on land because their flippers face backward.

Where do seals live?

Most seals live in cold waters near the Arctic and Antarctic regions. A few live in the Caribbean and Mediterranean seas and in the South Pacific. One kind of freshwater seal lives in Lake Baikal, in Russia.

How do seals hear?

Seals' ears have only a patch of wrinkled skin around an opening. Some scientists think seals use their hearing when they can't see. Like dolphins and bats, seals send out sounds that bounce against things and echo back. This may help them find holes in the ice in the dark.

Elephants on ice

Elephant seals

The largest seals are called elephant seals. They weigh up to four tons, or 8,000 pounds! Their noses are long and floppy. Southern elephant seals live near the Antarctic. You can see northern elephant seals in California.

Even small seals are heavy. Harbor seals weigh more than 300 pounds.

Eat and be eaten

Seals eat fish, shrimp, and squid. Some eat penguins and small sharks. Their enemies are large sharks, killer whales, polar bears, and walruses.

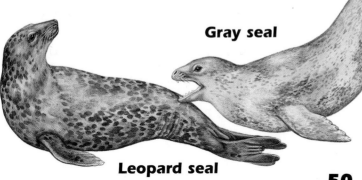

Gray seal

Leopard seal

SKUNK

Skunks are famous for smelling bad. But farmers need skunks to eat insects, rodents, and other pests.

Defense system

Skunks have two scent glands on their rear ends. They squirt smelly liquid, called musk, to protect themselves. The liquid also burns their enemies' eyes. Before they squirt, skunks give warnings. They raise their tails, hiss, arch their backs, or stamp their feet. The spotted skunk puts its hands up.

Striped skunk

Stripes, spots, and snouts

The North American skunk is black with two white stripes down its back. It can be found from Canada to Mexico. The hooded skunk lives in the dry southwestern United States and in Central America. The smallest skunk is the spotted skunk. It is the only skunk that can climb trees. It lives in deserts, plains, and brushy country of North and Central America. The hog-nosed skunk lives in the southwestern United States and in Central and South America. It has a snout that looks a little like a pig's.

Something upset this spotted skunk.

SLOTH

Sloths hang upside down most of their lives. They live in Central and South American rain forests.

Disguised

Sloths have small ears and flat faces. They live alone and don't make noise. They feed at night. They are nearly invisible by day. Their shaggy brown fur may be slightly green. That is because algae sometimes live there. So may moths, beetles, and mites.

A sloth uses its rear leg to hang upside down from a tree limb.

Counting toes

Sloths' front limbs are longer than their back limbs. Three-toed sloths have three toes on all four limbs. Two-toed sloths have two toes on their front limbs. Their back limbs have three. Sloths have sharp claws and teeth. They fight back if they feel threatened.

Slowly, slowly

Sloths are good swimmers. But on the ground, they have to crawl. Their legs aren't strong enough to hold up their bodies. They weigh up to twenty pounds. They use their claws to pull themselves along. This makes them easy **prey** for jaguars and eagles. In fact, sloths are the slowest mammals. But they're not lazy. Their bodies work very slowly. It can take a month for a sloth to digest a meal. Sloths eat leaves and other tree parts.

SQUIRREL

Squirrels live nearly everywhere in the world. Most are slender, with bushy tails and four big front teeth.

Lots of cousins

There are 225 kinds of tree and ground squirrels. The one you are most likely to see is the American eastern gray squirrel. Ground and tree squirrels look alike. Ground squirrels **burrow** into the earth. Some can survive in the desert, and others live in the cold **tundra**.

Squirrels must gnaw on things to keep their ever-growing teeth short.

Flaps of skin help this squirrel glide from tree to tree.

Can squirrels fly?

Some squirrels have a thin, furry skin that connects the sides of their bodies to their front and hind legs. They are called flying squirrels. But they don't fly like birds. Instead, the flaps help them glide from tree to tree. There are thirty-five kinds of flying squirrels in North America, Europe, Africa, and Asia. The African scaly-tailed squirrel can glide up to 1,500 feet. That's as far as five football fields placed end to end.

Home sweet homes

The tree squirrel lives in a nest in a tree hollow. Sometimes it builds other nests of leaves. The leaf nest is a sort of squirrel dining room. There, squirrels eat green leaves, seeds, nuts, berries, fruits, and insects.

TIGER

Tigers are big striped cats. They live only in Asia. Bengal tigers are the most numerous.

Almost extinct

Tigers are **endangered**. Three kinds have become **extinct** in the last seventy years. Only a few hundred Siberian and Sumatran tigers live in the wild today. There are less than thirty South China tigers.

A tiger's sharp teeth quickly tear into its prey.

Fierce hunters

Tigers hunt at night. In the dark, they can see six times better than humans. Tigers prey on deer, pigs, cattle, and goats. They can leap fifteen feet. They catch their **prey** with sharp claws. After a forty-pound meal, a tiger may not eat again for days.

Loners

Tigers stay with their mothers for about two years. This is the only time

Tigers are born in litters of 2 to 6 cubs.

tigers live in groups. After that, they live and hunt alone, in their own territories. Tigers mark their areas with scent or by scratching trees.

Show your stripes

Stripes help tigers hide in the tall grass or rain forest. Most tigers are red-orange or pale yellow-brown. They have dark stripes. Some tigers are white with chocolate stripes. A few are black with lighter stripes. White tigers don't live in the snow, as you might expect. They live in India.

WALRUS

Walruses are large mammals that live on the edge of the Arctic ice pack. They have big whiskers and two long tusks.

How do walruses float?

Like seals and sea lions, walruses have thin coats. Underneath is a layer of fat, called blubber. This keeps them warm and helps them float. Walruses also have pockets inside their throats. Filled with air, these pockets help walruses float. When they want to mate, males make noises with their air pockets. The noises sound like ringing bells.

Huge beasts

Walruses are larger than sea lions but smaller than elephant seals. Some weigh 3,000 pounds. Females weigh less. Walruses eat clams and other shellfish. They need about 6,000 shellfish a day.

Family life

Walruses breed far out at sea. Females give birth to one walrus pup at a time. Pups drink their mothers' milk for about two years. After mating, adult females take their young hundreds of miles north to pass the summer. A few males go, too. They swim for a week, then rest for a day or two. Much of time, they float on blocks of ice.

Once overhunted, walruses are again growing in numbers.

WEASEL

The many kinds of weasels include stoats, ferrets, fishers, martens, mink, polecats, and big wolverines.

Fancy fur

Weasels are valued for their fur. Ermines, mink, sable, and wolverines make warm, beautiful coats. To protect them, there are laws about how many can be captured. Mink raised on farms are slaughtered for their fur.

Stoat

Different coats, different colors

The stoat is a weasel that lives in Europe. It changes color twice a year. In the summer, the stoat has a brown coat with a white belly. In places where it gets colder in the fall, the stoat sheds its brown coat. A white one grows in. This animal is called an ermine. But it's really a stoat in its winter coat.

Ermine

What do weasels eat?

Weasels often live in burrows dug by other animals. They eat birds and small mammals, such as mice. A family of weasels may eat thousands of small animals in a year. They make nests with the fur of their **prey**. The black-footed ferret eats only prairie dogs. Ranchers consider prairie dogs pests. When they kill prairie dogs, the black-footed ferret has less to eat. Both animals could become **extinct**.

Read more about **Prairie Dogs** on page 43.

WHALE

Whales are mammals that live in all the oceans and seas. Their size alone makes them truly awesome.

How big can whales get?

The blue whale is the largest animal that has ever lived. Not even dinosaurs were as big. A blue whale is between 70 and 100 feet long. It can weigh up to 150 tons, or 300,000 pounds. Its heart is the size of a small car.

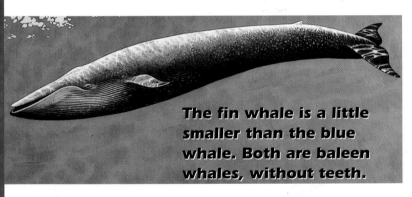

The fin whale is a little smaller than the blue whale. Both are baleen whales, without teeth.

Tiny food for big animals

The blue whale feeds mostly on tiny animals called krill. It eats one or two tons of krill a day. The roof of its mouth has a row of fibers, called baleen. When the whale takes a huge gulp of water, the baleen screens the krill out of the water.

Whales with teeth

Pilot whales, beaked whales, and white whales (sometimes called belugas) all have teeth. Toothed whales swallow fish and squid whole. The largest toothed whales are about sixty-six feet long.

How do whales breathe?

Whales rise to the water's surface to breathe. They exhale hard and inhale slowly. One breath can last nearly an hour. Baleen whales have two nostrils, or blowholes. Toothed whales have one.

A blowhole can spout water 20 feet or more.

WOLF

Wolves once lived all over North America, Europe, and Asia. Long overhunted, they are being brought back.

Gray and red wolves

There are only two kinds of wolves left. One is the gray wolf, or timber wolf. It looks a little like an oversized German shepherd. Gray wolves live in Alaska and Canada, and a small group lives in Mexico. A stable population of gray wolves lives in Minnesota. At least four other states have a few gray wolves. They also live in North Africa and South Asia. Red wolves are smaller than gray wolves. They live in Texas and Louisiana. They may be part coyote.

A pack of gray wolves chases a herd of bison.

Hunters in packs

Wolves spend most of their lives hunting. They prefer hoofed mammals like elk and deer. To catch one, a wolf can run at up to forty-five miles per hour for twenty minutes. Wolves also eat smaller mammals and fruit. They hunt in packs. Each pack has its territory. In the pack, only one pair of wolves has pups. This pair is called the alphas. They have from five to seven pups in a **litter**. While the pups are young, the father guards the den and the mother stays inside.

Wolves begin to hunt when they are several months old.

ZEBRA

Zebras are striped animals that live in Africa. They have bodies like horses and ears like donkeys.

The three Zs

Today, there are three kinds of zebras. All live in Africa. Grevy's zebras are the largest. Burchell's zebras are a little smaller. The smallest, the mountain zebra, lives in southwestern Africa.

Zebras' manes are short and stiff.

A young zebra can run an hour after it is born.

What's a quagga?

About 120 years ago, there were animals called quaggas. They were like zebras, but only their fronts were striped. They are **extinct** now.

Herd animals

A male zebra, or stallion, lives with a group of females, or mares. Their young are called foals. The dominant, or most forceful, mare leads the group. The lowest-ranking mare is last in line. Zebras may graze with antelopes, wildebeests, and ostriches. They are welcome because they eat the toughest grass. Each zebra has its own pattern of brown or black stripes. This confuses **predators**. When a lion or leopard looks at a herd of zebras, it is hard to tell the animals apart.

MARSUPIALS and MONOTREMES

Marsupials and monotremes are unusual mammals. Most live in Australia. Only one lives in the Americas.

Babies need extra care!

After marsupials mate, the **embryo** stays in the mother's body from twelve to thirty-seven days. Then a tiny baby crawls out of the birth canal. To survive, it must cling onto the mother's body and drink her milk. Most marsupial mothers have pouches with nipples, but some have no pouches. Their babies hang onto the nipple. Baby kangaroos stay in the pouch for about eight months.

Read more about **Koalas** on page 62.

Egg layers

Monotremes are egg-laying mammals. Like reptiles, they lay small eggs with tough shells. Monotremes keep a steady body temperature like other mammals.

Only two monotremes—the spiny anteater and the duck-billed platypus—survive today. The other kinds have become **extinct**. Monotremes have no nipples. The mother's milk oozes onto her fur, where the babies lick it up.

KANGAROO

Kangaroos are vegetarians. They live in Australia's deserts, grasslands, and rain forests.

Fifty nifty kangaroos

There are fifty kinds of kangaroos. The red kangaroo is seven feet tall. The gray kangaroo is human-size. The rat kangaroo is just a foot tall. Wallabies, wallaroos, quokas, and pademelons are also kangaroos.

A joey rests in its mother's pouch.

How do kangaroos hop?

Kangaroos are famous hoppers. Their back legs are long and powerful. They have short front legs. Long tails help them balance. The tails prop them up when they walk or stand.

Kangaroos have been known to hop as far as fifty feet.

At home in the pouch

The baby kangaroo is called a joey. It lives five weeks inside its mother's body. When it climbs out, it is the size of a honeybee. Its front feet have toes and nails. The joey uses them to crawl to a pouch on its mother's stomach. With its eyes shut, the joey finds a nipple in the pouch and sucks milk. It stays inside the pouch for eight months. For the next few months, it climbs out and back in again. When a joey is about a year old, it no longer fits inside.

KOALA

Koalas are picky eaters. They eat only the leaves of the eucalyptus tree. Of 350 kinds, koalas eat only 20!

Forest dwellers

Koalas are very gentle. They live mostly in trees. They sleep eighteen hours. They move about at night. Today, fires, cities, and farming have reduced the forest. Koalas have fewer places to live. Hunters killed hundreds of thousands of koalas for their fur more than 100 years ago. Hunting them is now against the law.

Baby koalas cling to their mothers.

Koalas need a lot of sleep.

Comfy pouches

Like kangaroos, koalas are hairless and tiny at birth. They nurse and grow in the mother's pouch. They climb outside when they are about six months old. But they come back inside to sleep and nurse. Baby kangaroos also hide in the pouch when they are frightened.

Riding piggyback

After koalas are too large for the pouch, their mothers still protect them. Mothers carry their babies on their backs until they are about a year old. They also feed their babies leaves that they have partly digested. Koalas live on their own when they are about a year and a half old.

OTHER MARSUPIALS

Opossum
Playing possum

Opossums are the only marsupials in the Americas. There are sixty-five kinds. Sixty-four live in South America. The common opossum lives in North America. It has gray fur and a long, hairless black tail.

When scared, opossums sometimes "play possum," or act dead.

Tasmanian Devil
Meat eaters

Tasmanian devils are bad-tempered. They have strong jaws, but they are not very fast. They eat small animals in a single gulp. They also enjoy roadkill. They live—you guessed it—in Tasmania, near Australia.

About one in ten Tasmanian devils reaches adulthood.

Wombat
Underground agents

Wombats are burrowing animals. They have big muscles and sharp teeth and claws. They can push through fences and hillsides. Their pouches face backward. This allows the mother to dig through the earth without getting dirt on her baby.

Wombats give birth to only one baby at a time.

SPINY ANTEATER and DUCK-BILLED PLATYPUS

Monotremes are mammals that lay eggs. The spiny anteater and the platypus are the only animals that fit that bill.

Odd ducks

The spiny anteater and the duck-billed platypus look odd, even if they don't look alike. Both animals pick up electric signals from their **prey**. They have special sense organs.

Good swimmers

Platypuses have been around for 62 million years. They have four webbed feet and feed in the water. They weigh about four pounds. They eat two pounds of crustaceans, mollusks, worms, and plants a day. They lay their eggs in burrows.

Spiny anteater

Duck-billed platypus

Spines for protection

Spiny anteaters have short legs with sharp claws. They are covered with hair and spines. If threatened, they roll into a ball with their spines out. Spiny anteaters live under rocks or in hollow logs. They hunt at night. With long, sticky tongues, they eat ants, worms, and termites. Female spiny anteaters grow a pouch when they are going to have a baby. They keep one egg there until it hatches. The newborn anteater stays in the pouch for about seven weeks.

BIRDS

Birds are the only animals with feathers. Their front limbs are wings. Most birds fly, but a few birds do not fly.

Lightweights

Birds have air pockets in their bodies and bones. This keeps them light and helps them fly. Feathers keep birds' bodies smooth and streamlined. This helps them move through the air. A bird's wings have very strong muscles. These are attached to the bird's chest. Flying makes it possible for birds to live in many different **habitats**. They can travel great distances. Some birds fly from one habitat to another with the seasons. We say they **migrate**. The Arctic tern migrates from the Arctic to the Antarctic and back every year, more than 20,000 miles.

Read more about
Eagles
on page 73.

Changing feathers

Tiny feathers, called down, keep birds warm. Larger body feathers shed water. These grow out of body pits called follicles. The follicles have muscles and nerves. They help move the feathers into the right position. When their feathers get ruffled, birds use their beaks to smooth them. Most birds **molt**, or lose their feathers, twice a year.

Giving birth

Birds lay eggs. Most hatch them in nests that they build. A nest can have as many as twenty eggs, or as few as one. Many young birds are eaten by **predators** or killed by bad weather.

CARDINAL, GOLDFINCH, and SPARROW

Cardinals, goldfinches, and sparrows are songbirds. Their feet are formed to perch on branches.

Robes of red

The male cardinal is bright red. The female is red and brown. Both have red bills, wings, tails, and head crests. They live in the eastern United States and Central America. They have a clear, cheery song. The female builds a nest alone. After the young leave the nest, the male takes care of them.

Cardinals

Finches of gold

Goldfinches live all over the United States and in southern Canada. The female is olive green, with a yellow throat and chest. In the summer, when it mates, the male is bright yellow. In winter it gets darker.

Goldfinches

Duller coats

There are more than fifty kinds of sparrows in North America. They have brown, gray, white, or pale yellow body feathers. Their bills are cone-shaped. Some song sparrows stay in one place year-round. Other song sparrows live in Canada in summer, then go to the southern United States in the winter. Each song sparrow learns to sing from another song sparrow. But every bird sings its own special song.

Sparrows

CROW

The crow's harsh call may not sound much like a song. But the crow is the largest of the songbirds.

Why do crows caw?

Crows have shiny, mostly black bodies. The common crow of North America is about twenty inches long. They are stout, with heavy bills. Their tails are squared off. Crows eat almost anything—even other birds. They feed in woods, farms, shores, cities, and suburbs. They call to each other when they find food or to warn other birds.

Crow

Crows to the rescue

Crows live in North America, Africa, Asia, and Europe. Owls, hawks, raccoons, and opossums **prey** on crows. But crows have an amazing defense system. When a crow is attacked, it cries out for help. Every crow that hears its cries will fly to help. Together the crows attack the **predator**. This is called mobbing.

Counting crows

Crows are very smart. They can count to three or four. Some can learn words, like parrots. They like to get together. Sometimes hundreds of thousands of crows roost together. The noise may bother people living nearby. On farms, crows are pests. They eat crops. That's why we have scarecrows. But crows are useful. They eat insects and **rodents** that do more damage than they do.

DOVE and PIGEON

Doves and pigeons are the same bird. There are about 300 kinds. The larger birds are usually called pigeons.

Lending a helping wing

In the Bible story about the Great Flood, Noah sent out a dove to find a sign of land. The ancient Egyptians ate pigeons. The Romans did, too. In Islamic lands, pigeons were protected by law. Many people have used them as messengers. Carrier pigeons can return home from great distances. Scientists think they use the sun and their sense of smell to find their way. They may also use the earth's magnetic fields. Pigeons have carried messages across battlefields in wartime. Today, people race them.

City pigeons

Pigeons in parks are descendants of the wild rock dove of Europe and Asia. The grayish brown mourning dove is smaller. It lives in much of North America. The reddish brown ground dove is even smaller. It lives in the southern United States and Mexico. Both male and female doves and pigeons give milk to their young. It comes from the crop, a little pouch in the throat. This milk is a lot like the milk of mammals. It is rich in protein and fat.

Mourning dove

Band-tailed pigeon

Rock dove, or common pigeon

DUCK

Ducks are web-footed birds that live in fresh and salt water. They live everywhere except Antarctica.

Quackers and waddlers

Ducks call to each other with many sounds. They have greetings, warnings, and take-off signals. Females quack. Males whistle, grunt, and coo. Ducks waddle because their legs are far apart and to the rear of their bodies.

Mallards

Birds of a feather

Ducks have waterproof feathers. Males are usually brighter than females. Baby ducks are born with tiny soft feathers called down. They follow the first moving thing they see after they hatch. This is called imprinting. Fortunately, the first thing they see is usually their mother.

Bottoms up!

Mallards are a kind of duck found all over the world. You may see them in the water with their tail feathers sticking up. They are feeding on plants and tiny animals just below the surface. The male has a bright green head with a white circle on its neck. The female is brown with a blue band on its wing.

Wood ducks

FLAMINGO, HERON, and STORK

Flamingos, herons, and storks are large wading birds. They have long necks and even longer legs.

Flamingo colonies

Flamingos are reddish orange, light pink, or white. Their flight feathers are black. They nest in groups, or colonies. Some colonies have 2 million birds! You can sometimes see wild flamingos in Florida. They don't nest there but in the Caribbean islands.

Flamingo

How do flamingos eat?

Flamingos' long bills turn down sharply at the end. To feed, they put their heads and bills upside down

underwater. With their thick tongues, they push muddy water through their bills. Tiny plants and animals are trapped inside.

Watch out for that bill!

Herons live in lakes and marshes. They may be gray, blue, brown, or white. They have sharp, daggerlike bills. They can spear food or use their jaws like scissors. They swallow whole fish, frogs, snakes, and mice. Herons nest in trees. They build colonies of many nests. The female lays three to seven eggs. Both parents feed the babies with food they have digested.

Great blue heron

Green heron

70

Stork

Storking around

There are storks on every continent except Antarctica. But most of them live in the tropics. They may wander from place to place looking for water. Most storks are black or white. Some grow pink feathers during breeding season. Storks build their nests in trees or on cliffs. They lay from two to five eggs. Their eggs hatch in thirty-two days. It takes baby storks from two to four months to learn to fly.

Great herons

Great blue herons live from southern Canada to Mexico. Their body feathers are gray-blue. They stand four feet high. Their wings are six feet wide, and they can take off from the water. They fly with their heads and necks folded back. Great white herons are white-colored blue herons.

Storks in America

Wood storks are the only storks in the United States. One group nests in Mexico. In summer it splits up and flies to Texas, Louisiana, Arkansas, Arizona, and California. The other group nests in Florida, South Carolina, and Georgia. It spends the summer in the Florida marshes. This **habitat** is getting smaller, and wood storks there are now **endangered**.

Great white heron

71

GOOSE and SWAN

Geese and swans are waterbirds with webbed feet. They are related to ducks, but their feathers are not as colorful.

Ganders and goslings

The female is the goose. The male is called a gander. Their young are goslings. Females and males have the same colored feathers. Some geese have been tamed, or domesticated. Long ago, geese were even used as guardians because they hiss at strangers.

Canada goose

Geese from Canada

You can watch migrating Canada geese as they fly south in V-shaped formations in the fall. In the spring they fly north. Today, more Canada geese stay put in suburban lakes and ponds. They are adapted to this new **habitat**. Canada geese have black heads, necks, and tails. Their bodies are brown.

Big and heavy birds

There are eight kinds of swans. All but one are white. The black coscoroba swan weighs only seven pounds. That's light, for a swan. The trumpeter swan of Alaska, Canada, and the western United States weighs about forty pounds. It's the largest of the birds that **migrate** long distances. Swans mate for life. Together, they raise their young, called cygnets.

Female swans are called pens. Males are called cobs.

72

HAWK and EAGLE

Hawks and eagles are birds of prey. They hunt during the day. Most mate for life.

Soaring and gliding

In the sky, hawks and eagles rise with warm columns of air, called thermals. It doesn't take much effort. Once the birds stop rising, they glide. Hawks and eagles may glide for thousands of miles when they **migrate**. They travel from Canada to the **tropical** forests of South America. It takes less than a month.

Golden and bald eagles

Not so bald

The bald eagle is the only eagle native to North America. It is the symbol of the United States. The bald eagle isn't actually bald. It has white feathers on its head and tail. Its body is dark brown. Its eyes are pale, and its beak is yellow. The sharp talons on its claws are black. Bald eagles live in the woods along streams. Like other birds of **prey**, they eat fish and small mammals. They have no natural **predators** except humans. It is against the law to hunt eagles.

Marsh hawk   **Red-tailed hawk**   **Swainson's hawk**

73

OSTRICH

Luckily for the ostrich, it doesn't need to fly. It is too heavy to get off the ground, but it can run very fast.

An odd-looking bird

With its skinny legs and long neck, an ostrich can grow eight feet tall. All its weight is in its feathered body. Inside is a very long intestine. The ostrich needs it to digest all the food it eats. This includes grass, leaves, fruit, and even lizards.

The ostrich's inner toes hold up most of its weight.

An ostrich's eyes have heavy lashes, for protection from dust.

The bird's neck has few feathers.

Where do ostriches live?

Ostriches live in eastern and southern Africa. Wild ostriches live in grassland or semi-desert areas. Others live on ostrich farms. There they are protected, and their long, beautiful feathers are harvested for fancy hats and costumes.

OTHER BIRDS THAT DON'T FLY

EMU

What's the second largest flightless bird?

After the ostrich, the emu is the largest flightless bird. It may stand five feet tall. Such a bird weighs about 150 pounds.

The active emu

Emus can run very fast. They also swim. In Australia, where emus live, farmers think of them as pests. That is because they often knock down fences and trample wheat looking for insects to eat.

An emu eats beside her chick.

A kiwi is the size of a hen.

KIWI

Another noisy bird

Like most flightless birds, the kiwi makes its own special noise. It sounds like a shrill whistle. In New Zealand, where it lives, the Maori people heard this noise from the forest. It sounded like *kee wee*. So they named the bird "kiwi."

PENGUIN

Another bird that doesn't fly is the penguin, which lives in Antarctica. There, the land is covered with ice. Instead of a nest, father penguins use their feet to keep their chicks warm.

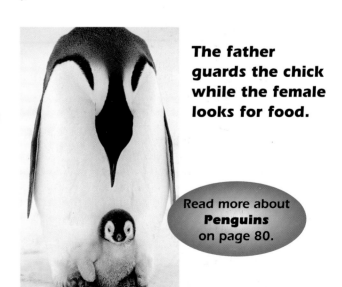

The father guards the chick while the female looks for food.

Read more about Penguins on page 80.

OWL

Owls are birds of prey. They live everywhere in the world except Antarctica. There are about 130 kinds.

Feathered all over

Owls have been around for millions of years. They perch straight up. Their faces are flat. Their wide eyes have feathers in a circle facing out. Their necks, ears, and hooked beaks are all covered with feathers. Owls' eyes never move. They are the only birds that blink. They lower their top lid. To close their eyes to sleep, owls raise their bottom lid like other birds.

Owls often frighten predators.

Busy hunters

Owls have to hunt a lot. They feed two or three times a night when they can. The bigger the owl, the bigger the prey. Owls eat small mammals, reptiles, amphibians, insects, and earthworms. Larger owls eat rabbits and opossums. They swallow everything. The bones and feathers that they can't digest form little pellets. Owls spit these up.

Rotating heads

Owls can turn their heads almost all the way around. They can also turn their heads upside down. This helps owls see and capture their **prey**. They see very well, by night and day.

The northern spotted owl's habitat in the northwestern United States is endangered.

76

PARROT

True parrots, macaws, parakeets, and lovebirds are all parrots. There are other kinds, too.

Bright colors

Parrots are smart, friendly birds with large heads. Two of their toes face forward. Two face backward. This helps them climb trees and grab seeds to eat. Parrots come in many colors. Some are bright red, yellow, or blue. Most are green. A few are dull in color.

Parroting people

Parrots are often loud and noisy. When kept as pets, they sometimes mimic human speech. This is probably because they are kept away from other birds. Wild parrots don't imitate people.

Six parrots: 1. Rainbow lory
2. Scarlet macaw
3. Red-tailed cockatoo
4. Thick-billed parrot
5. Masked lovebird
6. Slaty-headed parakeet

Many parrots

Most kinds of parrots live in South America. Others live in Africa and India. Some live in the mountains of Asia and Mexico. The Carolina parakeet is the only parrot that ever lived wild in the United States. It became **extinct** over the last 100 years.

Large and small

The hyacinth macaw is more than three feet long. It comes from Brazil. It has a long fancy tail. The smallest parrots are pygmy parrots. They are four inches tall and live in New Guinea.

PEACOCK

In North America peacocks live only in zoos and private yards. Wild peacocks live in Asia and Africa.

Blue and green

Peacocks are large pheasants. The blue peacock lives in and around India. The green peacock lives in Southeast Asia. The rare Congo peacock lives in Africa. It is blue and green. Peacocks make a lot of noise. They sometimes frighten away monkeys and deer. Tigers **prey** on peacocks.

A peacock tries to impress a peahen.

Showing off

In courtship, the male peacock is dazzling. His train feathers are three feet long. He shows them off by lifting his tail feathers underneath. The train takes up lots of space, forming a semicircle behind him. Some trains reach eight feet wide and five feet high. Train feathers have shiny "eyes" of blue and bronze.

Peahens

Females are called peahens. Their feathers are much duller than the males'. Their long tail feathers don't fan out the same way. One peacock lives with several peahens. The peahens lay four to eight eggs. These are about three times bigger than chicken eggs.

78

PELICAN

Pelicans are strong swimmers and graceful divers. They have deep pouches under their lower jaws.

How do pelicans catch fish?

Pelicans eat fish and crustaceans. They may dive for their food from the air, or while swimming. Sometimes pelicans cooperate with each other to feed. They swim toward the shore in a line. The fish swim ahead of them. When the fish reach shallow water, the birds scoop them up.

A pelican looks for a meal.

Down and up

The American brown pelican flies above the water until it sees a fish. Then it dives or spirals down. Next it plunges underwater to grab the fish. Finally, it bobs back up to the water's surface.

Many habitats

Some pelicans grow up to six feet long. Their wings are ten feet wide. Pelicans live in lakes, swamps, lagoons, and along the coasts. They live on every continent except Antarctica. Pelicans that live in a cool **climate** usually **migrate** to someplace warm in the winter.

A tall tale

Most pelicans are white or grayish. They sometimes have darker wing tips. Some pelicans have a reddish spot on their breasts. This made some people believe that the mother stabbed herself to feed her young with her blood. But this is a myth.

PENGUIN, PUFFIN, and SEAGULL

Seagulls visit beaches everywhere. Penguins and puffins swim in cold waters. Both are clumsy walkers.

Dressed for success

Penguins' tiny feathers are tightly packed. They look like fish scales. Feathers keep penguins warm in cold waters. The front feathers are white. Underwater, they are hard to see. The back feathers are black or blue-gray. They blend into the water's surface. Penguins' feathers help them hide from their main enemy, the leopard seal.

Big penguins

Weighing sixty pounds, emperor penguins are the largest penguins. They have purple bills. Their front feathers look golden.

A penguin dad protects his chick.

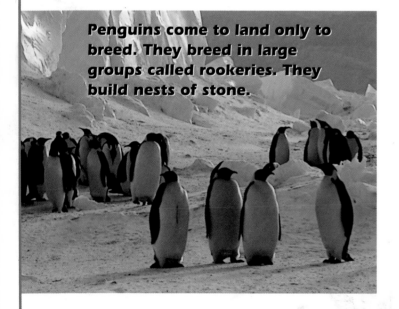

Penguins come to land only to breed. They breed in large groups called rookeries. They build nests of stone.

Caring dads

Taking care of an egg in the cold is hard work. The male looks after the nest all winter long. He doesn't eat for two months while the female feeds at sea. When she returns, the chicks hatch. She spits up fish to feed the new chicks.

Sea parrots

Puffins are shorter than penguins. Most puffins are about a foot tall. Atlantic puffins live in the Atlantic Ocean as far south as Maine and Iceland. Tufted and horned puffins live in the Pacific Ocean from Alaska to California. Puffins have triangle-shaped beaks. Some people call them sea parrots. Puffins use their beaks to catch lots of small fish. The colors of puffins' feathers help them hide in the water and on land. Their biggest enemy is the black-backed gull.

Atlantic puffins live on the coast of Maine.

Diving and flying

Unlike penguins, puffins can fly. Flying is hard work. The puffins have to beat their wings 300 to 400 times a minute. Puffins can dive up to eight feet. On land, they dig burrows with their claws to lay their eggs.

Seagull scavengers

Seagulls look for food along ocean shores. They eat both dead and live fish. They also eat garbage. Many people think seagulls are pests. But seagulls help keep beaches clean. Seagulls change color a few times in their lives. Their feathers are mixed when they are born. Then the birds turn gray or brown. Adults are usually white, with gray tips on their wings.

Black-backed gull　　**Herring gull**

ROADRUNNER and CUCKOO

Cuckoos live everywhere except Antarctica. The roadrunner of North America is also a cuckoo.

That's my baby

The common cuckoo goes *cuck-oo, cuck-oo,* like a clock. It lives in Europe and Asia. It lays its eggs in other birds' nests. Other birds may even hatch the cuckoo's young. The cuckoos of North America build their own nests.

Two cuckoos

Black beak, or yellow?

There are two main kinds of cuckoos in North America. The yellow-billed cuckoo gives a line of clucks. The black-billed cuckoo sings hundreds of soft notes. These birds are about a foot high. They live in woodlands and brushy shrubs.

Beep beep

The roadrunner is about twice as big as other cuckoos. It has a long tail and a rough crest on its head, with patches of red and blue behind each eye. The roadrunner makes different sounds. It crows, chuckles, clacks, and coos. It rarely flies. Instead, it runs fast on long legs. Roadrunners live in deserts. They eat snakes, scorpions, and other small animals.

Roadrunner

ROBIN

There are many kinds of robins around the world. A new yellow-breasted kind was found in Africa in 1998.

American robins

American robins have a reddish orange breast. The tops of their bodies are dark gray. They are about ten inches tall. Males sing *cheerup, cherrily, cheerup, cheerup; cheerup, cheerily*. Females call to each other and chatter. American robins live all over North America. If their summer home turns cold, they fly south for the winter. If it's warm enough, they stay. Once robins lived only in the woods. Now they live around houses, too.

A robin takes a bath in a puddle.

Blue eggs

Robins' nests are cup-shaped. They build their nests out of mud and grass. The female lays up to three sets of blue eggs a year. These sets of eggs are called clutches. When they hatch, the male feeds them. Baby

American robin

robins are very hungry. They eat 100 times a day! Robins eat lots of worms. They also eat cherries and grapes. Some eat tiny mollusks, fish, and even snakes. Robins are born without feathers. Their first feathers are gray. After they **molt** for the first time they look like adults, only duller. Young robins get their adult feathers after they mate once.

83

VULTURE

The vultures of North and South America are called New World vultures. They are kin to hawks and eagles.

Graceful in the air

Turkey vultures are also called buzzards. They range from Canada to South America. Their wings may span six feet. They are graceful flyers. They glide with their wings in a V-shape. Vultures flap their wings only to catch rising columns of hot air, called thermals. Their keen senses of smell and sight help them find food. Turkey vultures feed on dead deer, cattle, and sheep.

Long necks help vultures dig for meat.

Black flappers

Black vultures live farther south. They glide with their wings flat, not in a V. They flap their wings often when flying.

Endangered!

The California condor is also a vulture. Among flying birds, only the Andean condor of South America is larger. The California condor's wings are ten feet wide. Once, it was almost **extinct**. Zoos helped bring it back. Today, there are more than 150 California condors.

Hungry vultures feast on a carcass.

WOODPECKER

Woodpeckers hammer on trees with their strong, straight bills. They are looking for insects and sap to eat.

Made for the trees

All woodpeckers have short legs and sharp claws. Their two outer toes face backward. The middle two face forward. Woodpeckers have very long tongues. Sometimes the tongue has barbs. It is often very sticky. This helps woodpeckers capture bugs to eat. Woodpeckers spend most of their time on the sides of trees. Sometimes the male is drilling a nest. Some woodpeckers nest in live trees. Others prefer dead trees.

A crest of red

The top of any bird's head is called the pileum. The pileated woodpecker gets its name from the large red crest on its pileum. It lives in the eastern half of North America and in the Pacific Northwest.

Where do woodpeckers live?

Woodpeckers live almost anywhere there are trees. But none live in Australia or Madagascar. In North America, downy woodpeckers live in forests and suburbs. They are about six inches high. They are black and white on top and white below. The male downy woodpecker has a red patch on his head. The yellow-bellied sapsucker is a woodpecker, too. It lives in Canada and the eastern United States.

The pileated woodpecker can grow to be 20 inches high.

REPTILES

Reptiles are egg-laying animals with dry, scaly skin. They include turtles, lizards, snakes, and crocodiles.

Reptiles then and now

Tens of millions of years ago, reptiles were the most important animals on the planet. They lived everywhere. We call them dinosaurs. Most of these are **extinct** now. Today's reptiles come in many sizes and shapes. The python is the longest. This snake may grow up to thirty-three feet long. The leatherback turtle is the heaviest. It weighs 1,600 pounds. The dwarf gecko is the smallest. It is less than an inch long.

Cold-blooded

Reptiles are described as cold-blooded. This doesn't mean their blood is cold. It means that they don't heat their blood inside their bodies. They need heat from the outside, usually from the sun, to warm their bodies. Some reptiles **hibernate** in winter. All reptiles lay eggs. Their eggs have tough shells. Young reptiles hatch from their eggs fully formed.

A crocodile gets some sun.

ALLIGATOR and CROCODILE

Crocodiles and alligators float in slow-moving waters. Sometimes only their eyes, nostrils, and tails show.

Long and heavy

Crocodiles can open their mouths in the water without choking. A valve closes their throats. In West Africa, dwarf adult crocodiles grow to about five feet long. American crocodiles and Nile crocodiles can be twenty feet long and weigh a ton. In Southeast Asia, some saltwater crocodiles reach thirty feet!

Crocodile

What do crocodiles eat?

Crocodiles usually hunt at night. If they are hungry, they hunt by day, too. They eat frogs, birds, small mammals, and fish. The saltwater and Nile crocodiles eat deer, antelope, and hogs. Crocodiles also attack humans.

Alligator life

There are two kinds of alligators, the American and the Chinese alligator. Chinese alligators are about four feet long. American alligators are twice as big. They live from North Carolina to Texas. Both kinds of alligators dig deep holes to **hibernate** during the dry season. Alligators rarely attack humans.

What's the difference?

When crocodiles close their jaws, a long tooth sticks out on either side. Some people call this a smile. Alligators' teeth don't stick out. Also, modern alligators are smaller than crocodiles.

Alligator

Crocodile

LIZARD

There are 3,000 kinds of lizards. They include iguanas, Gila monsters, geckos, chameleons, and Komodo dragons.

Just warming up

Lizards live in **tropical** or **temperate** climates. The first thing most lizards do in the morning is warm up. They find a safe, sunny spot and lie around for a few hours. Lizards are big insect eaters. Lizards have smell organs in their tongues. Some lizards' tongues are even longer than their bodies!

Anoles of many colors

Anoles are the most common lizards in North and South America. The green anole lives in the southeastern United States. It can change from green to brown to yellow. It can also show patterns. Males have a pink growth at the throat, shaped like a fan. Green anoles grow up to eight inches long.

Leapin' lizards!

Most lizards have four legs and a long tail. A few walk on two legs. Others move like snakes. Some lizards live on the ground. Others live in trees. Flying dragons glide among the trees using skin flaps on the sides of their bodies.

Komodo dragons may be ten feet long and weigh 300 pounds. They live in Indonesia and eat small deer, goats, and bush pigs.

Iguanas

There are 700 kinds of iguanas. Most of them live in the tropics of North and South America. The common iguana lives in tropical forests, near rivers and streams. It is bright green. These iguanas can grow to five feet long. As an iguana ages, its skin gets duller.

Iguana

Gila monster

Poisonous lizards

The Gila monster and the beaded lizard are the only poisonous lizards. The Gila monster lives in the American Southwest and Mexico. The Gila monster is dark brown, with patches of pink or orange. Beaded lizards live only in western Mexico.

What's that noise?

Geckos squeak, click, croak, and bark. Other lizards make only simple sounds. There are 400 kinds of geckos. They live in trees and move about at night. They are brown, gray, or green.

Banded gecko

Chameleons

Chameleons live in trees from Spain to southern Africa to India. When threatened, some lizards change body color to hide. Chameleons do not. They get aggressive. They turn bright yellow or green.

Chameleon

SNAKE

Most snakes live in warm places. Some live near the Arctic Circle and the southern tips of South America and Africa.

Lots of varieties

There are more than 3,000 kinds of snakes. Most snakes aren't poisonous. But a few are. Australia is the only continent that has more poisonous snakes than harmless ones. In North America, there are about twenty kinds of poisonous snakes.

Garter snake

Big mouths

Snakes have no legs. Most have only one lung. Also, snakes are meat eaters. They swallow their food whole. Their jaws can open very wide. Some snakes lay eggs. Others give birth to live young. Newborn snakes live on their own.

Garter snakes

There are more garter snakes in North America than any other kind. They can be found from Canada to Costa Rica. Garter snakes live in almost every **habitat**. On top, their skin is brown, black, or reddish. It has checkerboard patterns. Most garter snakes have stripes running down their bodies, too. Near water garter snakes eat amphibians. On land they eat worms and insects.

A snake is coiled up in a tree, waiting for its prey.

Rattlesnakes

There are fifteen kinds of rattlesnakes in North America. In the United States, they live in every state but Maine. The interlocking rattles on a rattler's tail are left over from old skins. Rattlesnakes **molt** several times a year. Each time they molt, a rattle is left. Sometimes they break off, so you can't tell how old a rattler is just by counting its rattles.

Rattlesnake

Python

Python

Pythons come in many sizes. The smallest are about three feet long. Asian pythons grow to thirty feet. They may weigh 300 pounds! Pythons have fangs in the backs of their mouths. They kill by squeezing. They coil around their prey. Each time the animal breathes out, the python squeezes tighter. Finally, the prey suffocates and dies.

Watch out!

Rattlesnakes are poisonous. They often have more than two fangs in their mouths. New fangs grow in before old ones fall out. Rattlesnakes are called pit vipers. They have little holes, or pits, on both sides of their heads. These pits have glands that help the snake find its **prey**, even in the dark.

Scaly skins

Snakes' bodies are covered with scaly skin. Their skin doesn't grow with their bodies. When the skin gets too small, the snake molts. Its big underside scales overlap. These scales are called scutes. They help snakes move along the ground or up trees.

TURTLE

Turtles are reptiles with bony shells around their bodies. They are black, brown, or dark green.

What's a tortoise?

Turtles that live on land are often called tortoises. They have high-domed shells, stumpy legs, and small feet. Most turtles move slowly on land. Turtles move faster in the water. Sometimes they stay under for several days. If they **hibernate**, they may stay under for several months.

A tortoise moves slowly.

Between two shells

Turtles have two shells. The top shell is the carapace. It has about fifty bones, locked together. It includes the backbone. The bottom shell is the plastron. It has nine bones. The edges connect to the carapace. Outside the shell is a layer of skin. On top of the skin are scales called scutes.

Map turtles are named for their lines and spots.

Defending themselves

Turtles' shells protect them from otters, raccoons, crocodiles, bears, and large birds. Some turtles can pull their legs, tails, and heads inside their shells. Box and mud turtles can do this. But the snapping turtle can't. So it defends itself in other ways. It takes powerful bites with its strong jaw. Its tail has a ridge of spines.

FISH

Fish live almost everywhere there is water. They live in oceans, lakes, rivers, ponds, swamps, and little pools.

Many, many kinds

Altogether, we know of 21,000 different kinds of fish. That's more than all the mammals, reptiles, and birds together. More are being found all the time. Scientists think there may be another 7,000 kinds we don't yet know about.

Read more about **Salmon** on page 98.

Streamlined

Water is denser, or thicker, than air. Fish are shaped to move through water. They may be long and sleek, narrow, or even flat. Most fish have fins and a tail that help them swim. A slimy body coating helps fish glide along. It also protects them. Many fish have scales on parts of their bodies, too.

On the move

Some fish spend all their lives in one place, swimming in icy or warm waters. Other fish swim thousands of miles from one place to another. And some live in both the salty ocean and in freshwater rivers.

How do fish breathe?

Like people, fish need oxygen to live. They get oxygen from water, which has oxygen in it. The water comes into the fish's mouth. It is filtered through gills behind the fish's head. The gills keep the oxygen, but the water passes out.

CARP and CATFISH

Almost half of all the fish in the world live in freshwater. There are many, many kinds of freshwater fish.

Carp

Carp can live in muddy or polluted water. If the water dries up, they burrow in the mud. There, they find tiny plants and animals to eat. A female carp may lay 2 million eggs. They hatch in two to three days. Carp live in Europe, Asia, Africa, and the United States. Some are eaten as food. Goldfish are a kind of carp.

A carp feeds along the bottom of a river.

Leopard catfish

European catfish

Walking catfish

Upside-down catfish

Fish with whiskers

Catfish have spikes, called barbels, on their faces. Barbels look a lot like whiskers, which is why people said these fish look like cats. Catfish have smooth skin and forked tails. Most of them live in freshwater. The blue catfish lives in the Mississippi River. It can weigh 100 pounds.

OTHER FRESHWATER FISH

GAR
Blending in

Gars are long and slender. Their jaws are long, too—sometimes twice as long as the rest of their heads! Their skin has thick diamond-shaped scales. Gars blend in with the grass in slow-moving water. The spotted gar has black spots on its olive-brown skin. The longnose gar is dark olive on top. Its belly is white, and its fins are yellow-brown. It lives mostly in the Florida Everglades.

Longnose gar

PIKE
A popular fish

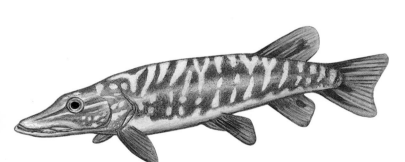

Pike are long fish with flat snouts and sharp teeth. Some weigh fifty pounds. People like to fish pike for sport. In North America, pike live from Alaska to Missouri. They also live in Asia and Europe.

Northern pike

PERCH
The long and short of it

Perch come in many sizes. The one-inch darter is a perch. The walleye is a perch but resembles a trout. It is three feet long. The yellow perch is about a foot long and weighs about a pound. Perch live in North America and Europe.

Blunt-nose trout-perch

EEL

Eels are long, snakelike fishes. They live in both salt and freshwater. Some live very deep in the ocean.

What makes eels different?

Most eels have two pairs of nostrils and no scales. They have no pelvic fins. Other fins may grow together. Also, their tails are pointed. Electric eels can make electric charges. This charge can kill a small animal.

A moray eel shows its teeth.

Freshwater eels

American eels live in freshwater from eastern Canada to Florida. They have small scales in their skin. They are dark brown or green. They sometimes grow to nearly five feet. American eels lay eggs in the ocean.

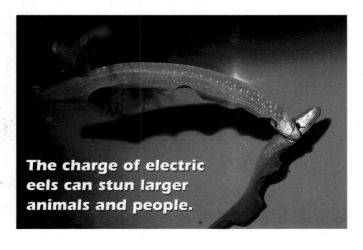

The charge of electric eels can stun larger animals and people.

Morays

Moray eels live around rocks and reefs in warm seas. Sometimes they are very colorful. Green morays have blue-gray skin. They look green because yellow algae live on their skin. The chain moray is dark brown, with yellow marks that look like chains. The goldentail may be dark, with small yellow dots. Or it may be pale pink with brown splotches. But be careful! Morays are dangerous. They may bite with their sharp teeth.

RAY and SKATE

Rays and skates have skeletons like sharks. They are made of cartilage, not bones. A few live in freshwater.

A lot alike

There is very little difference between rays and skates. Both are found in all the oceans and seas of the world. Skates and most rays live on the bottom of the sea. Their fins are round or diamond-shaped. Their mouths are on the bottom. Rays and skates sweep over their **prey** and start to eat.

Southern stingray

Weapons

Most rays and skates have long, thin tails. They use them as whips. Torpedo and electric rays stun their prey with electric charges. Stingrays have poisonous glands in their spines. The sawfish has a six-foot saw with lots of teeth. It uses its jaw to stir up the sand or to hack its prey.

Giving birth

No one knows when rays breed, or how long it takes their young to develop. They give birth to live young. Skates lay eggs in hard, black cases. They are usually rectangles. Some have long threads or curly horns. These tangle in seaweed, keeping the case safe from harm. It may be fifteen months before the eggs hatch. You may have seen these cases on the beach. Some people call them mermaid's purses.

A skate swims along the seafloor looking for food.

SALMON and TROUT

Salmon and trout swim mainly in rivers, lakes, and streams. Some migrate to the ocean after they spawn.

The journey home

Salmon mate at about three years old. They leave the cold seas where they feed and head upstream to the place where they were born. No one knows how salmon find their home stream, but they do. Scientists think a chemical code may guide them back home again.

Chinook salmon

Sockeye salmon

Mating dance

To mate, females vibrate their tail fins to loosen gravel. With the male, they do a courtship vibration. This creates a nest. Thousands of eggs and sperm drift to the bottom. This is called spawning. Atlantic salmon spawn for several seasons. Pacific salmon spawn only once. The difficult upstream journey home kills them.

Colorful trout

Trout mate in streams, too. They come in many beautiful colors. The rainbow trout is metallic blue on top. It has a red band on its sides. The brook trout has a red or yellow tint and wavy lines on top. There are red spots with blue halos on the sides. Even the brown trout has red and orange spots.

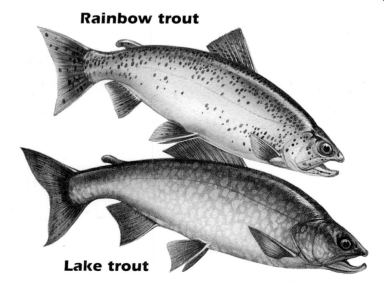
Rainbow trout

Lake trout

SALTWATER FISH

Fish live at every depth in the world's oceans. Those at the deepest parts may never come to the surface.

Tuna

Tunas are torpedo-shaped. They swim up to forty-five miles per hour. Usually, they swim in groups called schools. The tuna you eat from a can is probably a skipjack, bigeye, or bluefin tuna. These tuna swim in both the Atlantic and Pacific oceans. The heaviest bluefin ever caught weighed nearly 1,500 pounds.

Tuna

Sea basses

Sea basses are perchlike fishes with large mouths. They have teeth on their jaws and in the roofs of their mouths. They live in the Caribbean, the Gulf of Mexico, and the Atlantic and Pacific oceans.

Sailfish

Swordfish

Swordfish have long snouts. Their top jaws form a sword. They have no teeth. Swordfish eat crustaceans, squids, anchovies, and other fish. They are hard to catch. Many people use nets and harpoons to catch swordfish.

Sailfish

Sailfish have swords for snouts, too. But their swords have teeth. The middle rays of a sailfish's fin stick up, making a sail. The largest sailfish are more than nine feet long. They may grow six feet in their first year. Sailfish are the fastest fish in the ocean. They can swim sixty miles per hour. They live in the Caribbean, the Gulf of Mexico, and the Atlantic and Pacific oceans.

SEA HORSE

The sea horse is an unusual fish. It swims upright. To stay still, it wraps its long tail around coral or plants.

Great dads

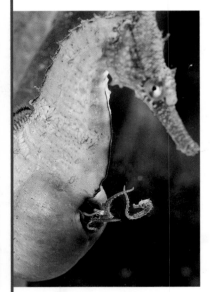

Baby sea horses being born.

Male sea horses are the most caring of all animal fathers. Sea horses mate for life. They do a dance that lasts for hours. Sometimes sea horses turn fluorescent when they dance. The female puts her eggs inside a pouch in the male's body. In two or three weeks, baby sea horses are born.

What do they eat?

Sea horses eat all the time. Their favorite meal is brine shrimp. But sea horses have no teeth, so they swallow the shrimp whole.

Over-fished

Conservationists worry that sea horses are over-fished. Each year 20 million of them are used in herbal medicines. They are used to treat asthma, heart disease, and other ills.

Disguises

Sea horses swim in warm, shallow water. They hide by changing color to match their background. They let other animals settle on them. They even grow skin that looks like algae. To us, a sea horse's head looks like a knight on a chessboard.

A female (right) and a male with 200 babies in his pouch.

SHARK

Shark! Just the word is scary. But sharks don't hunt people. People are invading their habitat.

What's cartilage?

Sharks are unusual fish. Their skeletons are made of cartilage. Cartilage is tough but not as hard as bone. You can feel it on the tip of your nose. Sharks' skin feels like sandpaper. It is covered with tiny scales like teeth.

A shark on the lookout for prey.

A born hunter

The shark is a killer. It has four, five, or six rows of teeth. When one set wears out, a new one grows in. The shark's mouth is on the bottom of its head. So are its nostrils. The shark's snout is blunt. It can sense the muscles moving in a bony fish.

Always on the go

Sharks must move to keep from sinking. They have up to eight fins. Fins help them keep their balance. Sharks keep their mouths open a bit. Water rushes in. It passes through the shark's five gills. The gills take oxygen from the water.

Mealtime

The shark eats large fish and other sharks. The smell of fish excites a hungry shark. It usually circles its **prey**. Sometimes it stuns a fish with its tail. Then it takes a bite. Or it may swallow its prey whole. A great white shark can swallow a twelve-foot shark. The shark's only **predators** are other sharks.

TROPICAL FISH

There are warm, tropical waters north and south of the equator. Many colorful fishes swim there.

Two by two

Butterfly fish have small, disk-shaped bodies. They are very thin from side to side. Butterfly fish often travel in pairs. Four-eye butterfly fish have two real eyes and two spots that look like eyes. They are white with black lines and swim in the Atlantic Ocean, the Caribbean, and the Gulf of Mexico.

Fish with beaks?

Parrot fish get their names from their mouths. Their teeth are joined with something like a beak. Parrot fish nip at algae and scrape sponges off the sea bottom. They are noisy when they feed. The rainbow parrot fish is orange in front and green behind. The body scales are green with orange edges. Its teeth are green, too.

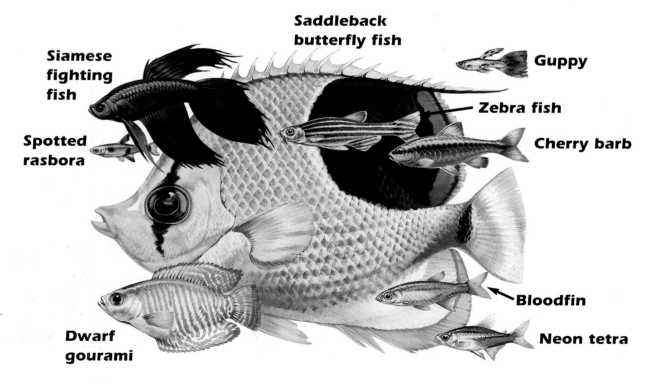

Saddleback butterfly fish

Siamese fighting fish

Guppy

Zebra fish

Spotted rasbora

Cherry barb

Dwarf gourami

Bloodfin

Neon tetra

Flat on the bottom

Flounders are flatfish. They settle on the bottom of the ocean. Both eyes are on the left side of their bodies. Gulf flounders are speckled and can hide in the sand. They live in the Atlantic from North Carolina to Florida and in the Bahamas. They also live in the Gulf of Mexico and the Caribbean.

Colorful angels

Angelfish are shaped a lot like butterfly fish. They are usually larger. The blue angelfish has a blue-tan body. Its scales have yellow edges. Its fins have fleshy lobes with yellow tips. It swims in the Atlantic Ocean and the Gulf of Mexico.

Millions of gobies!

Gobies live all over the Caribbean and the Gulf of Mexico. The smallest are one inch long. The longest are about nineteen inches. There even more gobies than blennies. Most have two back fins. The violet goby has a purplish brown, eel-like body. The frill-fin goby has rays on its top fin. It can jump from one tide pool to another.

Many blennies

Blennies live in shallow waters of the Caribbean and Gulf of Mexico. They are small with large eyes. They have fleshy tentacles on their heads. These are called cirri. There are many, many kinds of blennies.

A young angelfish shows its colors.

MOLLUSKS

Mollusks can be as small as a grain of sand. The biggest mollusk of all is the giant squid.

No bones about it

Mollusks have soft bodies with no bones. All their organs are covered by a mantle. The mantle is like a skin. Sometimes the mantle makes a shell for the animal. Other times, it is the animal's only protection.

Shallow and deep

Mollusks live in freshwater and oceans. Some live near the shore. Others live so deep in the ocean that people once thought they were **extinct**. Whales, fish, and walruses feed on mollusks. But their worst enemies are humans. People have killed too many mollusks for food. Even worse, they have polluted the waters where mollusks live. They have damaged the mollusks' **habitats**. Scientists are trying to find ways to help mollusks survive.

This squid glows in the dark.

Read more about **Squid** on page 106.

Arms and feet

From the outside, mollusks don't look alike. For example, clams and oysters have two-part shells. Snails, slugs, abalone, and conchs have a single, coiled shell. Octopuses and squids have none. But all of these animals have some sort of foot. It is made of muscle. Snails use it to move. Clams dig with it. The "feet" of an octopus are actually its arms. It uses its arms to grab its **prey**.

CLAM, OYSTER, and MUSSEL

Oysters, and mussels spend all their lives in their shells. The shells have two sides, called valves.

Filter feeders

People can barely see what oysters, clams, and mussels eat. Water enters their bodies through a small tube.

Hairlike body parts keep the water moving. Then the water is filtered through the animal's gills.

Oysters can change from male to female.

Bits of food are caught inside. The food is swept into the animal's mouth. The water passes out again.

Blue mussels sit among frilled anemone.

Clam it up

Clams have a foot made of muscle. It helps the clam burrow in the mud or sand. The clam

This Pacific clam has its foot out.

leaves a tube above the surface to let water in. Male and female clams release their sperm and eggs into the water, where they meet.

Where do oysters come from?

Oysters live in shallow waters. Adults attach themselves to another object. Their bottom shell is usually flat. The fleshy body stays in the upper shell. Males pass sperm cells into the water. They may **fertilize** eggs in a female's shell or outside it.

OCTOPUS and SQUID

The octopus and its relative, the squid, are spineless creatures. They are among the world's oldest animals.

How big are they?

Most octopuses and squid are small. But octopuses thirty feet wide do exist. And the largest animal without a backbone is a fifty-seven-foot squid!

"Octo" means "eight"

Octopuses have soft bodies with eight arms around a very large mouth. Their eyes have many parts, including a lens that moves. Experiments show that octopuses can see objects and tell one shape from another.

Octopus

Moving along

Octopuses move in several ways. Many use the suckers on their arms to crawl over the bottom of the sea. Some octopuses deep in the sea have skin between their arms. They move by opening and closing like an umbrella. Other octopuses take water into their bodies and then shoot it out again. This propels them through the water. Squid move this way, too.

Defense department

Both animals have a sac that contains black ink. They shoot this liquid into the water to confuse their enemies. They can also change body color.

Do squid have arms or legs?

Squid have five pairs of arms—ten in all. Four pairs are used for swimming. One longer pair captures other animals. Both the squid and the octopus eat meat.

SNAIL and SLUG

Snails and slugs live on land and water. Snails have spiral shells. Slugs don't have shells at all.

Twisted creatures

A snail begins life with its body balanced left and right. Before it becomes an adult, it twists its body and its shell. The snail brings its back end and the shell's opening forward. Now it can enter its shell headfirst and protect its head. This puts its gills out front. These take in oxygen from the water or air in front. Most of the snail's body remains inside the shell.

A snail and its eggs

What do snails eat?

Most snails graze on algae and tiny plant cells. But a few snails that live in the ocean **prey** on other shellfish. They have a poison that can bore through another animal's shell.

Moving like a slug

Snails and slugs have a muscular foot. It moves them along the ground or the water's bottom. The land slug lays down a slimy trail to give its foot something to grip.

Land slugs eat mostly plants. They often damage farms and gardens.

CRUSTACEANS

Crustaceans live in all of Earth's oceans. They also live in rivers, lakes, and ponds. A few live on land.

Hard shells

Crustaceans wear their skeletons outside their bodies. The skeleton isn't made of bone. It is made of a hard material called chitin. It does not grow with the animal. As the animal grows, the shell falls off, or **molts**. Underneath, a new shell is growing. It takes a day or two to harden. Until it does, the animal is in danger.

Mountain crab

Crustacean bodies

Crustacean bodies have three parts: head, **thorax**, or chest, and **abdomen**, or belly. Each part has at least two **appendages**. These appendages may be legs or antennae or breathing tubes.

Big and small

The smallest crustacean is the tiny water flea. The largest is the giant spider crab. It can measure twelve feet, from claw to claw. Krill look like tiny shrimp. They can live in the icy Antarctic Ocean. Copepods are so tiny you can barely see them. They float with other plants and animals. They feed on bacteria and parts of plants. Bigger animals, such as whales, eat these tiny animals. Large or small, all crustaceans lay eggs. Some look like their parents when they hatch. Others change how they look many times.

LOBSTER, CRAB, and CRAYFISH

Lobsters, crabs, and crayfish walk on ten legs. If one breaks off, they grow a new one.

Lobster life

Lobsters live on the bottom of the sea. If they escape fishing traps, some may live for forty years. Most lobsters' two front legs are claws. The smaller one slices dead fish. Lobsters like eating dead fish.

American lobsters are big business.

A crayfish takes a walk.

Crayfish

Crayfish live in ponds and streams. They look like small lobsters. They hide under rocks by day and feed at night. Then they eat small fish, snails, insect **larvae**, and worms. Some people use them for fish bait.

Where do crabs live?

Crabs usually live in the sea, too. But some crabs live in freshwater. Others live on land. Two kinds of crabs climb trees!

Crabs' claws can break clam shells.

Crabs eat small fish, worms, or whatever they can find at the sea bottom. The robber crab climbs palm trees to eat coconuts.

AMPHIBIANS

Amphibians are land animals. But they spend part of their lives in the water. Their skin is usually smooth.

Where do amphibians live?

Amphibians live everywhere on the Earth except Antarctica and Greenland. Frogs have the most **habitats**. Some live in deserts. Others live in **rain forests**. Still others live in ponds. Salamanders live in ponds, too. Others live in moist leaves or under rocks and logs. Salamanders and newts like **temperate** climates. They live mostly in North America, Europe, and Asia. Caecilians live in the **tropics**. They have no arms and legs, but they have backbones. They **burrow** in the mud.

Frogs may peep, bark, or even grunt.

Reproducing

Nearly all amphibians lay eggs. Frogs lay the most. The males **fertilize** them in the water. When the eggs hatch, tadpoles are born. Tadpoles are **larvae**. They will change shape, or go through **metamorphosis**, to become frogs. Other amphibians go through metamorphosis, too. But a few amphibians hatch looking just like their parents, only smaller.

Red-spotted newt

FROG and TOAD

Frogs and toads are noisy. Their calls tell you when they are mating. The calls also warn rivals and scare enemies.

What's in a name?

Both frogs and toads have four legs. Frogs jump. Their back legs are very powerful. Toads hop or even walk. Frogs and toads have short, round bodies. A toad's skin is dry and warty. A frog's is moist and smooth. Both animals have large, flat heads, and no necks. Most have very long tongues. Their tongues can stretch out like a rubber band to grab an insect or a spider.

A toad's color is its disguise.

From eggs to frogs

Most frogs and toads mate near water. The female lays thousands of eggs in the water. The male covers them with his sperm. After they go away, the eggs hatch. Tadpoles come out. They have tails and gills. As they change, they grow legs and lungs. Their tails disappear. This change is called **metamorphosis**. Many tadpoles are eaten by fish before they grow up.

Where do they live?

Frogs and toads live in ponds, marshes, and **rain forests**. A few frogs can live in extreme cold. Some toads live in deserts. Many frogs and toads can change color to hide from **predators**. They may also have poison on their skin.

A frog crouches on some moss.

SALAMANDER and NEWT

Salamanders and newts are tailed amphibians. They may look like lizards, but they are not. Lizards are reptiles.

Not too hot, please

Most salamanders and newts live north of the equator. They prefer a mild **climate**. The biggest group of salamanders lives in the Appalachian Mountains of the eastern United States. The world's largest salamanders live in China and Japan.

Red-backed salamander

Red-spotted newt

Small, bright, and beautiful

Most salamanders are less than six inches long. Their skin may be red or yellow, brown or black. Some have spots of another color. Or they may have bars or stripes. Mucus glands keep the skin damp. Some newts have warts.

How are babies born?

Salamanders and newts are born in different ways. Sometimes eggs are **fertilized** inside the female. The baby may stay there until it is born. Other salamanders lay eggs. The male fertilizes them on water or land. These eggs change into **larvae**.

Eat or be eaten

Salamanders and newts have large mouths and eyes. Some have stretchy tongues for catching insects. They eat worms, too. Snakes, fish, and birds eat salamanders and newts. A frightened salamander may have poison on its skin for protection.

INSECTS

Insects live almost everywhere. They pollinate flowers. They make honey, wax, silk, and shellac.

What makes an insect?

Adult insects have six legs and a pair of feelers, or antennae. Most have two sets of wings. Their bodies come in three parts: head, **thorax**, and **abdomen**. The tough outer covering is the insect's skeleton.

Big changes

Most insects change many times from egg to adult. This is called **metamorphosis**. It means "change in shape." Butterflies and moths go through metamorphosis. Females lay many small eggs. Inside each egg is a caterpillar. It is called a **larva**. It hatches. The larva eats all the time. Mostly it eats green leaves. But some larvae eat grain or even a wool sweater. The larva outgrows its skin two or three times and sheds it.

Read more about **Butterflies** on page 116.

Preparing for flight

Next, the larva spins a silk covering, or cocoon. It wraps itself like a mummy. This stage is called a pupa. Inside the cocoon, the pupa is becoming an adult butterfly. Finally, the adult breaks out. Its body hardens. Its wings expand and get flat. Then they harden, too.

ANT

There are about one quadrillion ants on Earth.
(That's 1,000,000,000,000,000!) They live in colonies.

Founding a colony

Most ants are females. They work all the time and never lay eggs. Every colony has at least one queen. She has wings. In early adulthood, she flies off with a male ant. He puts sex cells into her body and soon dies. The queen founds a new colony wherever she lands. She lays one or two eggs each day and uses the male's cells to **fertilize** them.

Life in a colony

Every ant has a job. The soldiers defend the colony. The workers get food. They work in groups. They "talk" to each other by tapping their antennae or giving off special chemicals. If food runs short, the colony may move to another place.

Leaf-cutter ants drag new leaves home.

Ant power

Ants can carry fifty-two times their own weight. They eat insects that harm humans and crops. They improve the soil by breaking it up. But sometimes ants get into human food and buildings. And they can sting. Ouch!

What do ants eat?

Most ants feed on other insects. Many eat seeds. Others farm fungus on beds of decaying leaves.

BEE

Bees live everywhere but Antarctica. Many kinds of bees live alone. Other bees live in groups called colonies.

Buzzing around

All bees have two sets of wings. These wings can move up and down, forward and backward. This allows bees to fly forward, backward, and sideways. They can also hover in one place. Some bees dance, too. They dance in circles to tell other bees where the food is. They wag their tails to tell how far away it is.

Bee city

As many as 80,000 honeybees may live in one colony. They all have one mother. She is called the queen bee. The males are called drones. Their only duty is to mate with the queen. All the worker bees are females. They don't lay eggs, but they do have stingers. Usually, bees do not sting unless they are disturbed.

How sweet it is!

Honeybees collect nectar and pollen from flowers. Moving from flower to flower, bees collect pollen on their legs. They suck up sugary nectar with their long tongues. Then they carry it home in a special stomach. Back at the hive, the pollen is put into teeny baskets. The nectar is stored in tiny wax cells. Special chemicals turn it into honey.

A honeybee at work.

BUTTERFLY and MOTH

Butterflies and moths are some of the most beautiful insects. They live all over the world.

On the wing

Kite swallowtail butterfly

Most butterflies and moths are no more than one inch wide. Some get much bigger. Every butterfly or moth looks for a mate. Some butterflies travel toward the equator in the fall. They travel away from it in the spring. The monarch butterfly flies to Mexico or southern California in winter. It returns north to lay its eggs and die. Its babies finish the trip and start all over.

Colors bright and dull

Adult butterflies have colorful scales in beautiful patterns. Moths are duller. Their scales are looser. Adult moths and butterflies eat a liquid diet. They have a special feeding tube. They sip nectar, tree sap, or fruit juice. Some moths drink animal tears.

Monarch butterfly

I see you!

Like other insects, butterflies have two eyes with many small lenses. Each sees a part of what is ahead. The butterfly sees only two or three feet away. Some see certain colors. Butterflies may see only red and yellow flowers, for example.

Owl moth

116

FLY and MOSQUITO

The housefly, the fruit fly, the black fly, and the mosquito all belong to the fly family.

Spreading disease

Flies cause lots of human misery. They often breed in garbage and manure. Some flies carry millions of germs on their feet. Diseases like cholera and dysentery spread this way. Other flies spread disease by biting people and infecting them.

Housefly

Pest control

Many flies live their stages as **larvae** and pupae in human and animal wastes. Mosquitoes develop in water. Taking care of waste solids and water is one way to stop breeding. Chemicals called insecticides have been used to kill flies and other insects. But insecticides, such as DDT, often harm the environment. They poison fish and other animals.

Horsefly

Do all mosquitoes bite?

Adult mosquitoes feed on flower nectar. But females need blood to produce their eggs. They break the skin to suck blood. A mosquito bite may cause only an annoying itch. But many mosquitoes are deadly. They can carry diseases such as malaria, yellow fever, dengue fever, and viral encephalitis.

Flight control

Flies and mosquitoes have two filmy front wings. Heavy veins make the wings strong. Two smaller winglike organs help the insect balance. Mosquitoes have scales on their wings and bodies.

GRASSHOPPER

To escape an enemy, the grasshopper can hop twenty times its body length. It can also fly.

Getting away

The grasshopper has 900 muscles. That's 100 more than people have. Its back legs are very powerful. They help the grasshopper escape its enemies. It can jump to get away fast. If the weather turns bad or food runs out, thousands of grasshoppers may **migrate**, or move, together. They leap high into the air and fly on the wind. In a few days, they can travel hundreds of miles.

This short-horned grasshopper has antennae shorter than its body. Long-horned grasshoppers have much longer antennae.

Singing in the grass

Only male grasshoppers sing. They sing to attract females. But the sound doesn't come from their mouths. The short-horned male rubs his rough hind leg against the edge of a front wing. The long-horned male rubs the bottom of one front wing under the other front wing.

Lending an ear

Grasshoppers feel, smell, and taste with their antennae. Long-horned females listen with pads near their knees. Short-horned females have "ears" under their wings. If the female likes the male's song, she lets him climb on her back. He curls under her and leaves a package of sperm. It will **fertilize** every egg she ever lays.

LADYBUG

Ladybugs eat aphids and other insects that feed on plants. They have very big appetites. Gardeners love them.

Beetles, too

There are about 300 kinds of beetles. Ladybugs are beetles. Their outer wings form a shield. This protects their hind wings and their bodies. They can live under stones that would crush softer insects. This is true of most beetles. Ladybugs' backs are highly curved. Their bottoms are flat. If they need to fly, they must unlock their upper wings and unfold their hind wings.

Did you know?

During the Middle Ages, the ladybug was dedicated to the Virgin Mary. Christians sometimes even refer to her as "Our Lady."

Ladybugs are tough insects with big appetites.

Brightly colored

The largest ladybugs are not even half an inch long. Most are smaller than that. Still, they are easy to see. Many are red or orange and have dark spots. Each kind of ladybug has a different number of spots. One kind, the red milkweed beetle, has four black spots and streaks. The convergent ladybug beetle has thirteen black spots. Guess how many the two-spotted ladybug beetle has.

This ladybug is looking for an insect to eat, not for nectar.

119

OTHER INSECTS

Praying mantises are friends to humans, but cockroaches are a pest—no question about it.

Praying or preying?

The praying mantis feeds on other insects. Its front legs look like they are folded in prayer. But the arms make a trap. This is where the mantis grabs its **prey**. It eats crickets, young cockroaches, grasshoppers, and bugs. The female eats the male after mating. Baby mantises may even eat each other.

Praying mantis

Gardeners' helpers

Praying mantises live in the eastern United States, southeastern Canada, southern Europe, and northern Africa. Gardeners like them because they eat insects. But lizards, cats, birds, and skunks like to eat praying mantises.

Cockroaches forever

Cockroaches lived on Earth before the dinosaurs. Today, there are about 5,000 kinds of cockroaches. Most live in hot, **tropical** regions. They live under logs, rocks, and bark. Others live in palm fronds and ant nests. When it gets cold, cockroaches move in with people.

Filthy pests

Only a few kinds of cockroaches are pests. But there are millions of them. Three main kinds of cockroaches live in North America. They feed on garbage, dead insects, or human food. Their only **predators** live outside.

A cockroach munches on some bread.

ARACHNIDS

**Arachnids can look like insects, but they don't fly.
They also have eight legs—two more than insects.**

Tiny pests

Mites and ticks are the smallest
arachnids. Their bodies are like
sacks with only one compartment.
Both are harmful to people. Ticks
live on other creatures, including
dogs, deer, and humans. Ticks may
carry Rocky Mountain spotted fever
and Lyme disease. Mites feed on
plants and animals. Sometimes mites
damage crops and farm animals.
Some cause disease, too.

Daddy longlegs

Daddy longlegs have long, slender
legs. If an enemy bites one, it breaks
off. A new one will grow in when
this arachnid **molts**, or sheds its
skin. Daddy longlegs usually feed on
dead insects and fallen fruit. They
may look scary, but they're harmless.

A spider's web is a beautiful trap.

Spiders and scorpions

Spiders and scorpions carry venom,
or poison. Spiders inject it with their
jaws. Scorpions carry it in their tails.
We say that spiders spin silk. They
use it to catch their **prey**.

SCORPION

The scorpion's tail makes it look like a tiny lobster. But lobsters don't sting like scorpions do.

A good eater

The scorpion has clawlike arms on both sides of its jaws. It uses these to catch its **prey**. Then it grabs the prey with its jaws. Next, the scorpion raises its tail over its body. In the tail is a stinger. The sting poisons the prey. The jaws crush the body. The scorpion injects digestive juice. Then it sucks up its meal.

They like it hot

Scorpions do best in hot **climates**. They hide in the day. They come out to hunt at night.

Fast learners

Scorpions do not lay eggs. The female gives birth to baby scorpions. She carries them around for about two weeks. Then they are ready to hunt.

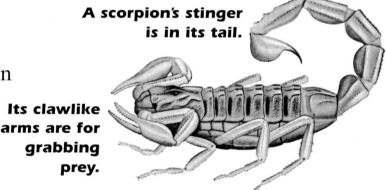

A scorpion's stinger is in its tail.

Its clawlike arms are for grabbing prey.

A mother scorpion with babies on her back.

Are scorpions dangerous?

Scorpions may attack if they are disturbed. A scorpion bite swells and hurts. Special medicine, called serum, usually makes the patient better. In the United States, one kind of scorpion can be deadly. It is tan with two black stripes.

SPIDER

Spiders are eight-legged creatures that spin a silky fiber. The silk can hold 4,000 times the spider's weight.

How do spiders catch food?

Most spiders spin webs to trap their food. Then they wait. The web of a garden spider is like a wheel. The spider sits in the middle. When it feels the tug of an insect, it knows lunch is served. It may kill the insect with its poison. Then it pumps digestive juices into the **prey**. This turns it into liquid, which the spider sucks out. Spiders eat many insects that destroy crops and carry disease.

Garden spider

Have no fear

Many people are afraid of spiders. Spiders are afraid of people, too. They usually play dead or run away when people come near. Spiders rarely bite people. Most spiders are not poisonous to people. But some widow spiders and tarantulas can be dangerous.

A wolf spider wraps her eggs in a silk cocoon and carries them with her.

Almost blind, but still alert

Most spiders have eight eyes, but they don't see well. They smell and hear poorly, too. In fact, the hairs on their legs are their best sense organs. They are very sensitive. They can detect the smallest motion.

GLOSSARY

Abdomen The back of three main parts of an insect, crustacean, or arachnid.

Altitude How high or low a place is above or below the ocean.

Appendage A body part that is attached to the main body of an animal.

Burrow (noun) A hole made for shelter. (verb) To dig into the ground.

Climate Regular year-round weather conditions. These include wind, temperature, and rainfall.

Embryo A baby animal before its birth, when it is still in its mother.

Endangered A term describing types of animals that are dying out.

Estivate To spend a period of time in a resting state to survive heat.

Extinct Types of animals that have died out.

Fertilize To make eggs or seeds reproduce by mixing male and female sex cells.

Gene A part in the cells of every living thing that determines how it grows and develops.

Habitat The place where an animal normally lives.

Hibernate To go into a deep sleep, usually for the winter.

Larva The form of some animals when they hatch from their eggs but before they become adults. The plural is larvae.

Litter A group of babies born at the same time and from the same mother.

Metamorphosis A change in an animal's form as it becomes an adult.

Migrate To travel from one place to another to breed or feed. The journey is called a migration.

Molt To shed an outer layer, such as hair or feathers.

Prairie An area with deep, fertile soil covered by coarse grasses but with few trees.

Predator An animal that survives by killing and eating other animals.

Prey (noun) An animal that is eaten by another animal. (verb) To seize and eat another animal.

Rain forest A tropical area of tall, broad leaf trees and high rainfall.

Rodent A mammal with sharp front teeth that must continue gnawing to keep its teeth from growing too long.

Temperate Regions with a moderate climate and four seasons—spring, summer, fall, and winter.

Thorax The middle part of the three main body parts of an insect, crustacean, or arachnid.

Tropical The region around the equator where climate is hot all year.

Tundra A plain without trees in cold regions. The layer below a tundra's topsoil is frozen all year.

INDEX